China's Struggle to Modernize

STUDIES IN
WORLD CIVILIZATION
Consulting Editor:
Eugene Rice
Columbia University

China's Struggle to Modernize

Michael Gasster
Livingston College, Rutgers University

Alfred A. Knopf   *New York*

THIS IS A BORZOI BOOK
PUBLISHED BY ALFRED A. KNOPF, INC.

Library of Congress Cataloging In Publication Data

Gasster, Michael, 1930–   , China's struggle to modernize.
(Studies in world civilization)
Bibliography: p. 147
1. China—History—1900–, I. Title.
DS761.G34 1972 915.1'03 74–39747
ISBN 0–394–31504–9

Manufactured in the United States of America

First Edition

9 8 7 6 5 4 3 2

Typography and cover design by Elton Robinson.
Cover map by J. P. Tremblay.

Cover art, detail from Ploughing by Shih Lu, courtesy of the
Prints Division, the New York Public Library, Astor, Lenox and
Tilden Foundations.

Preface

During the twentieth century China has made the most startling reversal of any country in history. For some three thousand years prior to 1900, the Chinese compiled an unmatched record of continuity. China's reputation for being "unchanging" was not deserved, but no people on earth surpassed the Chinese in devotion to the ideal of harmony and in the tenacity and pride with which they held to their tradition. After 1900 repeated waves of revolution battered the great wall of Chinese tradition, until at mid-century the ideal of "struggle" replaced that of harmony, and China became the world's most militant exponent of radical change. A revolution began, affecting the lives of 550 million people, more than one-fifth of the human race, in a land that only a few decades before had been commonly thought to be hopelessly stagnant.

In this brief introduction to modern China, I have attempted to outline the history of this dramatic reversal. Since the book is intended primarily for students in Western and world history courses, I have concentrated on certain topics that link China's modern history with world history. In particular, I have stressed the role played by those Chinese who were influenced by foreign ideas and who attempted to modernize their country. What were the sources of their ideas? How did they attempt to translate foreign ideas into solutions to Chinese problems? What difficulties did they encounter in trying to adapt their ideas to the realities of Chinese life, especially to the peasants' needs? How did they attempt to meet those difficulties?

China's struggle to modernize has included alternating efforts to reject, embrace, and compromise with Western culture and to preserve, destroy, and rejuvenate traditional Chinese culture. Haunted first by fear of Westernization (in the nineteenth century), and next by a fear that China would *fail* to Westernize (during much of the twentieth century), the Chinese in recent years have sought ways to become modern without at the same time becoming Western.

If this book achieves its purpose, readers will be led to ask new questions, including a large and fundamental one: Has China's reversal really been as dramatic as it appears? To such questions we shall offer only the most tentative answers, for they require extended discussion in a much longer and more technical book than this one. For this and other omissions there is consolation in the fact that no single book on China can touch on more than a fraction of her story. There is simply too much ever to be told. I shall feel amply rewarded if the small part I tell here encourages readers to consult the authors referred to in the text and Bibliography.

To those authors, and to others too numerous to name in a short list of references, I apologize for my attempt to enhance readability by omitting footnotes. By depending so heavily on their scholarship, I have taken the liberty of impressing them into service as virtual co-authors of this book. I absolve them of all responsibility, of course, for how I have represented their work.

Among my co-authors I wish to name my wife, Susan, who has selflessly read and reread several revisions of this manuscript. Her professional literary talents, critical gifts, and deep human understanding have been indispensable to me.

M. G.
New York, New York

January, 1972

Contents

Contents

Introduction

Professor Gasster's essay on modern China is one in a series of twelve paperbacks that Alfred A. Knopf, Inc., is publishing under the title *Studies in World Civilization*. Another published study, Frederick W. Mote's *Intellectual Foundations of China*, is devoted to traditional China. Of the ten other studies in the series, one book deals with early and one with modern developments in Africa, India, Japan, Latin America, and the Middle East. The purposes of the series are to introduce students early in their careers to the historical experience of peoples, societies, and civilizations different from their own; to provide a core of attractive readings for courses in World Civilization; and, at the same time, to furnish teachers of Western Civilization with comparative evidence from non-Western history deliberately selected to illuminate central problems in the Western historical experience.

One of the intellectual virtues of our time is a willingness to recognize both the relativism of our own past and present beliefs and the civilizing value of the study of alien cultures. Yet, in practice, as every teaching historian knows, it is immensely difficult to construct a viable course in world history; and almost as difficult to include satisfactorily unfamiliar, and especially non-Western, materials in the traditional Western Civilization survey course. The reason for this difficulty is that until very recently mankind had no common past. The pre-Columbian civilizations of America attained their splendor in total isolation from the rest of the world. Although the many different ancient peoples living around the Mediterranean were often in close touch with one another, they had little knowledge about civilizations elsewhere. The Chinese knew accurately no other high civilization than theirs. Until the nineteenth century, they regarded the ideals of their own culture as normative for the entire world. Medieval Europe, despite fruitful contact with the Islamic world, was a closed society; medieval Western historians identified their own past with the history of the human race and gave it meaning and value by believing that this past was the expression of a providential plan.

The fifteenth-century European voyages of discovery began a new era in the relations between Europe and the rest of the world. Between 1500 and 1900, Europeans displaced the populations of three other continents, conquered India, partitioned Africa, and decisively influenced the historical development of China and Japan. The expansion of Europe over the world gave Western historians a unifying theme: the story of how the non-Western world became the economic hinterland, political satellite, and technological debtor of Europe. Despite an enormously increased knowledge of the religions, arts and literatures, social structures, and political institutions of non-Western peoples, Western historians wrote a universal history that remained radically provincial. Only their assumptions changed. Before 1500, these assumptions were theological; by the nineteenth century, they were indistinguishable from those of intelligent colonial governors.

The decline of European dominance, the rise to power of hitherto peripheral Western countries such as the United States and the Soviet Union and of non-Western ones such as China and Japan, and the emergence of a world economy and a state system embracing the planet have all created further options and opened wider perspectives. Historians of the future will be able to write real world history because for good and ill the world has begun to live a single history; and while this makes it no easier than before to understand and write the history of the world's remoter past, contemporary realities and urgencies have widened our curiosity, enlarged our sympathies, and made less provincial our notions of what is relevant to us in the world's past.

One viable way to overcome the ethnocentric provincialism of an exclusively Western perspective is to deal with both Western and non-Western civilizations on a comparative basis. The comparative procedure has a double advantage. On the one hand, it describes a culture different from our own and makes clear to us that in order to understand it we must scan its history with humility and sophistication, abandoning implicit analogies with our own civilization and leaving aside some of our most fundamental assumptions about time, space, causality, and even about human nature itself. On the other hand, it encourages us to make explicit those very assumptions of our own tradition we now recognize to be different or unique. By studying comparatively an alien civilization we learn something about it—a good in itself—and at the same time sharpen our understanding of ourselves.

Professor Gasster's book serves these purposes admirably. It is at once a splendid introduction to the history of China in the late nineteenth and twentieth centuries and a penetrating study of modernization, that is, of the emergence in a non-Western society of characteristics which first became visible in the West in the eighteenth century. Before the Industrial and French revolutions Europe was itself "underdeveloped," closer in its modes of production, technology, class structure, demographic patterns, transportation, and communications to the Roman Empire in the age of the Antonines or to the Chinese Empire under the Mings than to a "modern" or "advanced" twentieth-century society. To observe in China, therefore, a process of modernization parallel to, and modeled on, the European is to learn to see the modernization of the West from a fresh and original point of view. Conversely, the problem of modernization gives the Western student a useful entrée to modern Chinese history. Since the model is Western, he will recognize in the Chinese experience some themes familiar to him from the history of his own civilization; but, since the men who adapted the Western model to their own needs thought and acted in a cultural context radically different from the European, the striking contrasts that he will meet between the familiar and the unfamiliar will alert him at once to what is unique in the Chinese historical tradition. Finally, it is precisely the complex developments we label "modernization" which have forcibly pushed both China and the countries of the West out of the parochialism of their traditional pasts toward participation in a common world history. The process continues to be a painful one, envenomed by aggression and resentment, punctuated by war and revolution. It is far from over. Professor Gasster usefully illuminates a critical phase of world history.

Eugene Rice
Columbia University

China's Struggle to Modernize

Chapter 1

The Modern World and Nineteenth-Century China

One day in 1945 a team of five Communist cadres* arrived in remote Stone Wall Village. Their mission was to start a revolution among its five hundred residents. They posted proclamations, called a meeting to explain the posters, and tried to speak privately with individual villagers. The cadres found themselves ignored, for the peasants were afraid of the landlord who dominated the village. Eventually a poor tenant farmer came to talk to two of the cadres. At last they persuaded him that his poverty was not due to his own shortcomings—"I guess I have a bad brain," he would say—but to the high rent exacted by the landlord. The farmer brought his friends to the discussions, and the group grew to thirteen. But news of the meeting reached the landlord, and one of the thirteen was murdered. The terrified peasants promptly ceased coming to meetings; the cadres, themselves shaken, were back where they had begun. But they persisted. Once again they turned to recruiting peasants. When finally the peasants' number grew to thirty, they invaded the land-

---

* The term "cadre," sometimes roughly translated "official" or "functionary," refers to someone who has received training in Communist methods of organization and leadership and who is considered qualified to exercise authority and assume tasks requiring initiative and responsibility.

lord's house and took him prisoner. For two days at mass meetings they accused the landlord of crimes and cruelty, and three days later seven hundred people (including visitors from nearby villages) participated in a meeting that ended with the landlord's death.

In the 1940s incidents similar to this one occurred in thousands of Chinese villages. Some peasants who had been brutalized, others who merely saw an opportunity for gain, and still others whose reasons we do not know were roused to deal peremptorily, harshly, and even savagely with landlords and officials. The peasants did not think they were engaged in a nation's "struggle to modernize." They were struggling, not to do anything as abstract as "modernize," but to survive—to eat and to be safe from bandits, undisciplined soldiers, greedy landlords, corrupt officials, and the vagaries of nature. But in their own way the awakened peasants, like the scientists experimenting in laboratories or the workers making steel, were fighting for modernization. Before 1900 peasants had often rebelled and killed, but never had such rebellions been part of a larger movement to change society in fundamental ways. After 1900 such larger movements developed and in the 1920s began to reach out to the peasants. Their struggle for survival became part of China's struggle to modernize; and, in turn, China's struggle to modernize became rooted in the countryside.

coalescence of the two struggles

In this gradual coalescence of two struggles, a crucial turning point was reached during the war against Japan (1937–1945), when urban intellectuals and workers went into rural areas to organize the resistance. The five cadres who came to Stone Wall Village included two intellectuals (a former teacher and a former student), a waiter, a shop assistant, and a farmer. Thus the cadre team in itself represented a combination of backgrounds and exemplified the new social cohesion that developed in wartime China; but even more important, the cadre team in its relationship to the villagers represented a new conception of politics and a new method of effecting social change.

The overturning of Stone Wall Village thus reveals in microcosm some of the main issues in China's modernization. And it suggests some important questions. What brought thousands of outsiders to isolated villages? What kept them going, sometimes for many weeks, in the face of the peasants' fear and silence? How did the cadres overcome their own fear? What finally made the hesitant peasants act? What happened to the cadres and the villagers and to the relationships between them once the landlords were gone and the villages went through land reform, collectivization, and communization? What does all of this mean for China's modernization? Perhaps we can begin to seek a few answers.

The incident at Stone Wall Village was originally described by correspondent Jack Belden in *China Shakes the World*. When that book was published in 1949, the title must have seemed odd, especially to Westerners, who were accustomed to shaking China rather than being shaken by her. For more than a century, China's weakness had been a fact of life. For several centuries a few Western nations had dominated world history. As Professor R. R. Palmer once wrote to explain why his history of the modern world dealt chiefly with Europe: "The main reason is that modern civilization has been formed by the expansion of ideas, institutions, and industries that originated in Europe. . . . The last few centuries may in fact be called the European Age, and while this age is probably now closing, it has produced the world as we know it today."

Few scholars in the West would take exception to this distinguished historian's view of the modern world. Indeed, it is by the familiar characteristics of this world that we often decide whether or not a country is "modern." Does the country have enough science, technology, and industry to outweigh traditional forms of knowledge and production? Does it have high-speed means of transportation and electronic communication, a high degree of literacy, and universal education? Do its farmers use chemical fertilizers and machinery, and do they produce for the market instead of only for their own needs? Do its political leaders have close contact with the masses, and do citizens feel a common bond with each other? Do people think that they have a reasonable possibility for having a different and better life than their parents and grandparents? If these characteristics predominate in the society, we regard it as a modern one. The point in time at which these characteristics begin to overshadow traditional ones is said to mark the beginning of a country's modern history. Measurement of such characteristics is difficult, but among the rough yardsticks used are the ratio of inanimate to animate power, per capita productivity, the number of people living close to or using railroads and other relatively high-speed means of transportation, and the number of people occupied in primary industries, such as agriculture, compared with those in manufacturing and service or administrative occupations.

The Chinese, like many other peoples in the last century, have attempted to increase their use of machinery and reduce their dependence on hand tools and human energy, to increase the amount that each person can produce, and to pierce their vast, undernourished interior with life-giving railways, roads, and airlines. But until very recently China seemed unable to effect such changes rapidly and efficiently or, indeed, to perform the most basic functions that a nation should—notably, feeding her people adequately. Despite vast natural resources and the great talents and energy of the Chinese people, change has been painfully slow in China.

One reason that change has been comparatively slow there is that China had a deeply rooted tradition of paternalistic leadership. Relationships between leaders and followers are central to any society, but in China those relationships, and especially the character and outlook of leaders, were the primary concern of the great majority of philosophers and statesmen for some two-and-one-half millennia. Questions of how to exercise leadership were central to thinkers at least as early as Confucius, and his successors grappled endlessly with problems of duty, social obligations, and conflicting loyalties. Eventually an elaborate social code developed that rested firmly upon family relationships and therefore reached into the very marrow of every Chinese. Each thought, word, and action was heavily influenced by an idea of what was proper between people of different stations. By the nineteenth century China was very much dominated by a small, privileged group, the so-called scholar-gentry, that claimed a position in society much like a father's position in the family. China's struggle to modernize can be studied by focusing on the emergence of a new generation of leaders that were dedicated to far-reaching change.

<u>Modernization in China required conscious, sustained, persevering, dedicated effort against the tide of history</u>. Although modernization has occurred nowhere without great effort, the historical obstacles, and therefore the effort required, were probably much greater in China than in Western Europe. But even if the problems were not actually greater, it is clear that in late-modernizing societies the role of leaders would be different. English leaders, if indeed they were conscious that they were engineering "modernization," had no example to study; Chinese leaders could learn from England, Germany, the United States, Russia, and Japan, and they could not avoid being more aware than English leaders of modernization as a conscious goal. <u>Another difference is that China undertook to modernize largely because imperialism threatened her very existence; modernization meant survival as a nation</u>. China's nationalistic leaders therefore felt a special duty to promote modernization. This feeling was particularly strong among intellectuals, heirs to deep traditional obligations both to serve society and to lead it.

Two ideas of Modernization

Twentieth-century Chinese leaders, especially intellectuals, have been heavily influenced by the West, but to them modernization has not necessarily meant the same as Westernization. Modernization is a process whereby a society *incorporates* the new ideas, practices, and institutions necessary for the mastery of science, technology, and industrial production. For the non-Western world, this process has included a certain amount of Westernization —by which is meant the *transplantation* of distinctively Western ideas, practices, and institutions. But modernization is not mere transplantation; it includes the rejuvenation of some traditional ideas and practices, the modification of what has been taken from the West, and the assimilation of outside borrowings to internal customs and conditions. (An interesting example is Japan, which surely has modernized; but quite a strong case can be made that Japan has not Westernized.) China's leaders, united in their determination to make their country modern, resist policies that tend to make China too Western. Thus Mao Tse-tung has said that China should assimilate foreign culture in order to "nourish her own culture," but he has rejected "wholesale Westernization." The Chinese, however, had not always thus distinguished the processes of modernization and Westernization. How they came to do so is a major theme in our story.

Author's Theme

IMPERIAL
CHINA

China has always been in touch with other peoples and subject to foreign influences. Contact with Central and Southeast Asia was maintained throughout recorded Chinese history. Indirect trade with Rome, by way of the Middle East, began in the second century B.C., and Buddhism came to China from India soon after. Chinese ships, which far surpassed European ships in size and construction, crossed the Indian Ocean to Africa almost a century before the Portuguese sailed to India. Through twenty centuries, China and Europe influenced each other relatively little, but China gave far more to the West than she took from it; similarly, she changed Buddhism more than she was changed by it. What is sometimes referred to as China's "isolation" must be understood as the failure of foreign influence to alter the basic style of her civilization, not the absence of foreign influence.

China knew no civilization higher than her own and had no conception that there could be such a civilization. To the Chinese, all foreign traders and emissaries were barbarians, and almost every contact they had with other peoples, from the nomads of Central Asia to such wide-eyed Europeans as Marco Polo, seemed to confirm their own superiority. Partly as a result of the deference paid to Chinese civilization by nearly all outsiders before the nineteenth century, the Chinese came to believe that the world had only one great culture, China's, and that all people should share in it. Thus she did not develop the idea of a world of nation-states dealing with each other on the basis of equality. As John K. Fairbank has put it, "China was a world in itself, not a nation among nations."

One of the most persistent themes in China's history is the strong effort to create and maintain an effective polit-

Chinese theme of effective government

8

ical unity. Long before China became an empire, the impulse to create a rational political order was already a potent force, and considerable thought was devoted to the best means of creating a viable system of government. As early as the second millennium B.C. the Chinese were beginning to develop an administrative center to which outlying villages were linked in a relatively systematic fashion. During the next thirty centuries, they accumulated a wealth of experience in political administration unparalleled in human history. The solutions they worked out varied according to changing circumstances, of course, but the Chinese have always been faced with certain recurring problems due to the size and diversity of their land and people. Centuries of dealing with these problems produced distinctive patterns of political behavior and organization. Clusters of villages and towns developed relationships among themselves that became increasingly difficult to modify. Individuals became accustomed to dealing with each other according to practiced means: Villages A, B, and C paid taxes to agents sent out from town X and settled disputes according to principles they and their forebears had long since determined were best. There were margins for diversification. Relationships were not the same in the north as in the south, nor in big cities and their surrounding countryside; but even variations were likely to be deeply rooted in ancient experience. Divergent local patterns sometimes had to be reconciled with the needs of central authority, such as when great armies had to be raised against invading nomads, but the thirty centuries had allowed time for many patterns of reconciliation to be woven.

China's traditional patterns of political unity were far from uniformly harmonious blends, but they had developed out of so much reasoned experimentation that nearly everyone had long since stopped thinking there might be a better alternative. The government was able to perform its essential functions reasonably well, and the people could only give thanks that life was no harder than it was. By late imperial times, according to one authority on the traditional Chinese state, "it was probably the most elaborate and sophisticated governmental system existing in the world in its time." During the Ch'ing dynasty (1644–1912) the system was more elaborate than ever because the rulers were Manchus, descendants of a neighboring tribe that had conquered China; as foreign conquerors who were a small minority in a huge land, they felt insecure and hence added many administrative devices to protect their rule.

Under what has been called imperial China's "centralized authoritarianism," power radiating from the national capital spent itself as it passed through provincial capitals on its way to the nearly 1,500 local administrative districts (*hsien*). A surprisingly small bureaucracy functioned with the help of many semi-official and unofficial aides and supernumeraries to balance but rarely to overcome centrifugal force. At the district level, power administered by bureaucrats gave way to a wide variety of local power relationships. The relationships were worked out, depending upon local conditions, among minor employees of the bureaucrats and various members of the local elite, including scholar-gentry, landowners, village elders, and other such prominent or influential people. Wealth was a source of power but so was education, and kinship was so important that a tightly knit clan could have influence that was out of proportion to its wealth and educational level. A shifting and uneasy balance was maintained among what was by 1800 a patchwork of administrative devices and informal local arrangements. Even when sewn as tightly as imperial rulers could manage, the administrative system was never all-encompassing; there were always countless communities in which little or no outside authority was felt. Elaborate as it was, imperial autocratic rule remained incomplete. Most people paid scarcely any attention to the central government and only a little more to *hsien* officials. They had very few contacts beyond family, clan, and nearby villages.

Administrative voids were filled, where they were filled at all, primarily by the scholar-gentry. These educated men, usually of some wealth, helped to manage local affairs that officials did not handle; some of them had been officials or would later become officials, and others derived an income from land they owned or from teaching. Their influence, security, and prestige were greatly enhanced by privileges they held (such as exemptions from certain taxes), by their close association with officialdom, and by their stature as learned men. Entry into this class, which constituted the highest social stratum in traditional China, was obtained primarily by success in the civil service examinations. Nearly everyone was eligible for the examinations, but since success required many years of rigorous training, the rich had a considerable advantage. The scholar-gentry was not a hereditary or entirely self-perpetuating group, and there were times when as much as 40 percent or more of its new members came from "commoner" status (that is, from families that had not had a scholar-gentry member for at least several generations). But, on the whole, the scholar-gentry exhibited a remarkably high degree of continuity in its membership, particularly since new members from commoner backgrounds shared or quickly came to share the values and general world view of the elite group. Thus a gulf existed between the scholar-gentry and the rest of the Chinese people.

The elite's active participation in local affairs helped to bridge the gap, and so did the power of certain Confucian principles. One principle was that educated men must serve society, and another was that they must set a good moral example. The latter principle strengthened the ties between upper- and lower-class values and institutions. A Chinese family head might feel that he bore the same relationship to his family as the court, officials, and scholar-gentry did to society as a whole. Ideally, government and family were based on the same principles.

These shared principles permitted the relatively effective functioning of the society, which was sharply divided between those who had wealth, power, and privilege and those who did not. Although approximately 0.5 percent of China's population dominated the other 99.5 percent, there were long periods of just rule and acceptable living conditions, to say nothing of the extraordinary achievements of Chinese civilization. Never in the history of the world did so few manage to dominate so many for so long. Hundreds of times, when domination became too oppressive or traditional arrangements failed for some other reason, the peasants rose in revolt, but only three or four times in two thousand years did they succeed in sending great dynasties crashing into oblivion. The old system was always restored, and the changes that were made were always heavily outweighed by the continuities.

By the nineteenth century traditional arrangements were failing more seriously than ever before. Peace, prosperity, and new crops had permitted the population to grow far beyond anything known in the past, and the delicate balance maintained by a resilient but always precarious system was upset. Size of farms shriveled, many had to be sold, hunger and disease spread, and millions existed in suffering, anger, banditry, and revolt. Not coincidentally, the quality of the Chinese leadership likewise declined. A succession of mediocre emperors reigned in Peking from 1796 on, and the entire administration became riddled with incompetence and corruption. In this forbidding climate, the European Age dawned for China.

changes in the 19th C for China

CHINA AND THE MODERN WORLD

Foreign traders coming to China had long been considered bearers of tribute. From the early sixteenth to the early nineteenth century European traders were similarly treated. As the Industrial Revolution accelerated, the ideas and economic needs of Westerners in general, and Great Britain in particular, could no longer be satisfied by the Chinese system of dealing with them as tributary states. The British came to regard free trade not merely as an economic necessity but as a law of nature. Government decrees, intoned one English exponent of laissez faire, "are erected against and opposed to the natural tendency of things and are in the end as absurd and ineffective as it would be to direct the winds by Order in Council, or to manage the tides by Act of Parliament." Business interests insisted on official support for their demands that China facilitate Western-style commerce. Meanwhile the British smuggled vast amounts of opium into China, inflaming the trade issue.

breakdown of Chinese economic + political framework

Thus China's economic and political system, which had been adequate to manage relations with all pre-industrial societies, could no longer accommodate changing British needs. Soon the Chinese belief that China was the entire civilized world also clashed with British national pride. War resulted in 1839, and Britain's victory in 1842 brought her traders most of what they wanted. Hong Kong became British, five ports were opened to trade, and in those "treaty ports" foreigners were allowed to live permanently, trade freely, and be governed by their own laws and courts.

Eventually more than eighty cities were opened to trade. There were also seventeen settlements in which foreigners could live, own property, preach Christianity, and govern by their own laws not only themselves but also the many Chinese who lived in these enclaves. Some of the settlements were sizable. The foreign settlement in Shanghai, for example, by 1928 measured 5,584 acres and had a population of 833,000; the separate French concession added another 2,500 acres and 297,000 people. Thus Shanghai alone had well over a million people living in foreign-controlled territory on nominally Chinese soil, and about 96.5 percent of them were Chinese. It was in such settlements that many Chinese first came into contact with foreigners. Increasing numbers of Westerners also began to travel into the interior of China, introducing their religion and their worldly goods, weaving new threads into China's intellectual, social, and economic fabric. China's tariff became subject to the control of Western powers, and she had to pay heavy indemnities for war damages; these two impositions seriously damaged her economy and her capacity to improve it. Chinese life became affected to an ever-widening degree by the presence of growing numbers of foreigners who lived according to their own customs, as defeat followed defeat in major wars and minor clashes throughout the century.

In addition to the disturbances connected with foreign relations, China found herself faced with urgent internal problems. Population spurted from about 150 million in 1700 to more than 300 million around 1800, and to 430 million by 1850. This caused a great strain on China's resources, economic system, and government machinery. The strains impaired the efficiency of production and distribution, tax collection, and government services. The cost of wars and defeats added further burdens. As the economy foundered and the government increasingly found its troubles unmanageable, popular protest spread. Outbursts against the government broke out here and there in China toward the end of the eighteenth century and with increasing ferocity and frequency in the first half of the nineteenth century. Rebellions in the middle of the nineteenth century, the most serious of which was the T'ai-p'ing* Rebellion (1850–1864), took perhaps 20 million or more human lives, more than perished on both sides in World War I; the destruction, chaos, and human misery can scarcely be imagined. The central government barely survived, shaking and enfeebled. Peking's grip on the country now loosened, as it was forced to yield power to provincial governors and military commanders, some of whom became at least semi-autonomous.

The concurrence of the series of defeats in foreign war that threatened China with extinction from outside with domestic turmoil that threatened her from inside created a dual crisis of gigantic proportions. It was in response to this dual crisis that China's leaders began to think there was a need for their country to change.

Self-strengthening movement

From 1860 to 1900, as the dual crisis deepened, the Chinese undertook many new experiments. They founded schools in which Western languages, mathematics, and science were taught; they studied international law, established a Western-style foreign office, and began to engage in Western-style diplomacy; they built arsenals and shipyards in which they could manufacture modern weapons and introduced new concepts into military training; they sent students abroad; and they began to think about adopting Western methods of transportation and communication. All that they did, however, they considered means of defense. Each step had to be justified on the grounds that it would help to keep the foreigners out; at the same time, each experiment had to be guaranteed not to impinge upon the essentials of Chinese life. Thus the founding of new schools had to be justified on the grounds that they would train diplomats who could outwit the Westerners and engineers who could design and build better weapons than the Westerners had; at the same time, the new schools had to enroll only students who already had sound traditional training and who would continue it—the new schools were to offer a supplement to, rather than a substitute for, older learning.

The policy governing such experiments was well ex-

---

* Pronounced *Tie-ping*.

pressed by the slogan Chinese learning for the fundamentals, Western learning for practical application. The "practical application," however, was clearly subordinate to the fundamentals, for whenever Western learning intruded too much upon Chinese learning the experiment was terminated. Between 1872 and 1876, for example, after years of proposals and many months of elaborate preparations, about 150 young Chinese were sent to England, France, and the United States to be educated. The 120 boys who came to America, most of them between the ages of twelve and sixteen, were supposed to stay for fifteen years, but they were rather abruptly ordered back to China in the summer of 1881. The chief reason given for terminating the project was that the students were neglecting their Chinese studies (which they were required to continue while abroad) and "indulging in foreign customs."

Chinese did not want to Modernize

The Chinese were primarily interested in preserving their own way of life, not in modernization. They remained confident that their own principles were valid and that Western superiority was confined to such peripheral matters as the manufacture of ships and guns. They would borrow nothing that might fundamentally alter their way of life. This program of moderate, defensive, traditionalist reform has come to be known as the "self-strengthening movement."

intellectual behind 100 days of Reform

Toward the end of the nineteenth century a few Chinese began to look at things differently. One man, K'ang Yu-wei* (1858–1927), even went so far as to suggest that the essentials of Chinese life were not incompatible with modernization; imaginatively reinterpreting traditional doctrines—too imaginatively, said critics who accused K'ang of distortion—he argued that Confucius himself had been a reformer and that adopting fundamentally new practices need not lead to Westernization. Few would listen to him, and even though the emperor was among the few, the effort to carry out a thorough-going reform program in the summer of 1898 lasted such a short time that the period has come to be known simply as the Hundred Days.

---

* Pronounced *Kong Yo-way*.

The attempt ended when reactionaries led by the Empress Dowager Tzu Hsi seized power and imprisoned the emperor. K'ang's heroic but quixotic foray into reform politics made only a brief ripple in the flow of nineteenth-century traditionalism. The overwhelming sentiment of Chinese leaders was that anything genuinely new would also be Western, and therefore innovation should be confined to peripheral and transient matters.

Traditionalism, however, was not the only massive barrier to modernization in nineteenth-century China. The West itself played a significant role. Chinese in the United States, especially laborers working in mines and railway construction all across the American West, were subjected to severe discrimination and brutality. Chinese students may have suffered much less than laborers, but they were also humiliated. In their case, Western double-dealing and race prejudice contributed to the failure of the experiment. Li Hung-chang* (1823–1901), during the last thirty years of his life probably the most influential statesman in China, had expected the United States military and naval academies to accept some of these boys when they completed preparatory school, since an 1868 treaty provided that Chinese and American students could enter each other's government schools. When the Chinese were rejected and when discriminatory immigration legislation and other anti-Chinese policies were adopted in the United States, Li found it difficult to answer the conservatives who demanded termination of the mission.

One possible alternative was to send more boys to Europe, where Chinese were accepted in military and naval academies. But there too they felt racism. A sensitive Chinese student in France, one of Li Hung-chang's protégés, wrote concerning praise he received from his professors:

This praise is also caused by the fact that Westerners have had little contact with us Chinese and usually are scornful of us. Therefore, whenever there is a Chinese student who knows a little and understands half of what he has studied, he is praised

---

* Pronounced *Lee Hoong-jong.*

as being extraordinary. This "being extraordinary" [as an individual] is just a sign of being despised [as a race].

It was not only the relative handful of Chinese abroad who encountered this sort of discrimination. Thousands more found it in the treaty ports and, as missionaries spread inland, increasingly in the countryside. A not uncommon reaction was that of the missionary S. Wells Williams, who lived in China for forty-three years and studied his surroundings carefully. He came to the conclusion that although the Chinese "have more virtues than most pagan nations" and although "there is something to commend, there is more to blame." Adding up their shortcomings he concluded that they "form a full unchecked torrent of human depravity, and prove the existence of a kind and degree of moral degradation of which an excessive statement can scarcely be made, or an adequate conception hardly be formed." Many missionaries did not allow their vision of pagan degradation to overshadow their humanitarian desire to bring peace and enlightenment to China, but others agreed with Williams that the Chinese "are among the most craven of people, cruel and selfish as heathenism can make men, so we must be backed by force if we wish them to listen to reason." When men who held such prejudices went among the Chinese people and preached Christianity, all the while claiming the protection of unequal treaties and Western armed might, Western culture could hardly commend itself as a model for China.

In brief, Chinese attitudes toward Western culture were mixtures of resentment and envy; traces of admiration were heavily outweighed by hostility. These feelings became more ambivalent as Western influence in China spread. Even though Western imperialism paralyzed such efforts as the Chinese made to modernize and Western racism offended them, a few Chinese began to imitate some features of Western life, in business and manufacturing as well as in clothing and religion. Some also went to work for Western firms, thereby obtaining experience they later put to use in Chinese firms; others began to invest in Western firms, thereby departing from traditional habits of investment in land or moneylending. By the 1890s there seemed to be hardly a feature of Western society that someone or other had not recommended China adopt—a parliament or some other sort of public forum in which to discuss affairs of state, innovations in newspaper publishing to provide information for discussion and a channel for criticism of the government, an alphabetic system to promote greater literacy, jury trials and other legal reforms, and nearly every conceivable type of economic reform, including measures to raise the social status of merchants. The divided feelings that governed such men were recorded by a Chinese educator who recalled his first trip to Shanghai as a teenager:

Shanghai by 1899 was a small city with a few thousand arrogant foreigners. But the city was well governed, with clean, wide streets and electric or gas lights. I thought the foreigners were wonderful. They know the secret of electricity. They had invented the steam engine and built steamboats. They took the place of my old gods who had melted away in the face of my instruction in science, and occupied my mind as new ones. At the same time they served as new devils, too, for their arrogance, coupled with clubs of the policemen, frightened me. In the list of regulations displayed at the entrance of a park on the banks of the Huang-pu River, Chinese as well as dogs were forbidden admission. This said much. The foreigner appeared to my mind half divine and half devilish, double faced and many handed like Vishnu, holding an electric light, a steamboat, and a pretty doll in one set of hands, and a policeman's club, revolver, and a handful of opium in the other. When one looked at his bright side he was an angel; on the dark side he was a demon.

In the nineteenth century the Chinese saw mainly the demonic side of the West. But as the century came to a close they began to feel an ambivalence that was to haunt them for many years to come.

Chapter 2

The Swing Toward Westernization 1900-1928

Around 1900 China paused at a fork in the road. Looking over its shoulder along the path of traditionalism, the government could see forty years of defeat. Ahead, clearly in view, lay almost certain disaster, for at that very moment China seemed about to be carved into bite-sized colonial portions. The Peking authorities decided to explore a new route, one that seemed to skirt the West by way of Japan. After 1901 Chinese modernization began to follow Japan's example.

Between 1895 and 1905 Japan had smashed China; thrown off some of the most obnoxious features of the unequal treaties that the Western powers had imposed on her; consummated an alliance with Great Britain, the world's leading power, on a basis of equality; and thrashed another prominent imperialist power, Russia, in a bloody war. It was a decade's work that aroused Chinese envy, particularly since Japan seemed to have borrowed a great deal from the West without sacrificing her own unique cultural identity. Japan had combined industrialism, modern military methods, and at least the appearance of constitutional-parliamentary government with a strengthening of the emperor's position and the destruction of feudal power. This combination made the enfeebled Ch'ing government, harassed for decades by the loss of its power to provincial military regimes, dream once again of restoring central authority and shoring up its defenses against the West.

Beginning about 1901, therefore, the government intensified its efforts to modernize the armed forces, build railroads and other modern means of transportation and communication, streamline its bureaucracy, promote modern education, and develop industry and mining. Some of its most enterprising steps were prompted by Japan's example. Among the most significant measures were the dispatch of thousands of students to Japan and the decision, reached in 1905 and 1906, to adopt a constitution. The students were to provide trained personnel for the government's modernization program. The constitution was a defensive measure undertaken in a spirit resembling nineteenth-century self-strengthening. The Empress Dowager reasoned that "the wealth and strength of other countries are due to their practice of constitutional government, in which public questions are determined by consultation with the people." For her, constitutionalism was not intended to guarantee individual rights or to limit government or to divide power or for any of the other purposes known in Western democracies; instead, its object was to make China wealthy and powerful. After several months of study the government decided to follow closely the kind of constitution adopted by the Japanese, who had borrowed theirs from Prussia. In the Empress Dowager's eyes, the artful combination of elected representation with strengthened imperial prestige and power was among the most attractive features of the Japanese constitution.

The decision to study foreign governments in order to determine what kind of political system would be best for China represented a remarkable change of attitude. Of their many great achievements, none had given the Chinese greater pride than their form of government, which for lengthy periods had functioned efficiently and justly, despite premodern conditions and problems of immense area and population. For the Chinese now to confess so openly that they had something to learn from foreigners about the art of government was an about-face of the first magnitude.

Thus, as the twentieth century began, the rotting Ch'ing dynasty was moving further than ever before toward rejecting Chinese tradition and adopting Western practices. But even as it quickened its pace along the new path, the government was already being overtaken by more radical competitors. To understand the new steps taken by the government and the still newer ones called for by others, we must look into the backgrounds of the new movements.

INTELLEC-
TUAL
FOUNDA-
TIONS OF
MODERN
CHINA

It is easy now to forget how novel and how enormously revolutionary—in the West as well as in Asia—was the idea that rapid social change is both desirable and possible. That life *should* be very different from what it had always been was an idea that people were beginning to accept in late nineteenth-century China. Still, the conviction persisted that great changes, even if they were desirable, were not really possible; it was difficult to see that life *could* be very different from what it had always been.

Yen Fu and the Idea of Progress   The man who did most to encourage confidence in the possibility of change in China was Yen Fu* (1853–1921). Yen came from a family of scholars and received an intensive education in the traditional style. His grounding in the Chinese classics, although solid, was abbreviated due to a reversal in the family fortunes resulting from the death of Yen's father in 1866. The youngster then entered a new shipyard school that offered cash prizes and subsistence allowances as part of its program to recruit able students. He spent five years studying mathematics, science, navigation, and, since it was the language of instruction, English. After graduation he made several training voyages to Japan and Southeast Asia, and in 1876 he was sent to England for advanced training. There his interests blossomed. Like a number of other Chinese in the time of the self-strengthening movement, Yen wanted desperately to know why Western countries were so much stronger than his own. For more than two years he pursued this question relentlessly, studying British society, government, and thought. By the time he

---

* Pronounced *Yen Foo*.

sailed for home in 1879 he felt that he had found some answers.

Yen kept his ideas to himself until China's defeat by Japan in 1895. Pained by his country's plight, Yen had to speak out; his countrymen, reeling from their defeat, were at last ready to listen. In a series of newspaper articles Yen compared Chinese and Western societies. The main differences, he found, lay not in technology or military science, but in the values and ideas. Of these, the major difference was that "The Chinese love antiquity but belittle the modern, whereas Westerners struggle to make the present better than the past; Chinese accept the ups and downs of order and disorder, prosperity and decline, as the natural course of the universe, while Westerners consider that daily progress should be endless."

Yen searched more deeply for an explanation of why Chinese and Westerners held such different attitudes, and the search led him into many blind alleys, reversals, and inconsistencies. But some ideas he found struck a responsive chord in many of his readers. One idea was that of competition. The Chinese stressed order, stability, and social harmony, whereas the Westerners believed there were benefits to be derived from struggle and competition. Westerners realized that life was a struggle for existence, that nature selected the fittest for survival, and that fitness was proved by success in competition; indeed, competition furthered fitness by bringing out the potential abilities of each individual. Competition tested a man's mettle and toughened him for further struggle and survival. Competition and struggle, therefore, were in Yen's view the keys to progress. Another idea was the utility of individual liberty. Men struggle in pursuit of their own individual interests, and, in their determination to satisfy their self-interest, individuals "grind and polish each other. . . . Beginning in mutual antagonism they end by completing each other." The genius of Western society was that it allowed men to exercise freely their abilities: it encouraged men to act and released their energies. Moreover it did so in such a way that the pursuit of self-interest resulted in the fulfillment of society's interests. Miraculously, Yen thought, Western society was so constructed that each man's struggle to improve his position added up to all men improving theirs. In brief, he marveled, "unity and progress result from diversity and competition."

Yen's lasting significance is that he introduced the ideas of Darwin and the classic British liberals to China at a time when the Chinese were ready to receive them. Just when the Hundred Days ended and just when Confucianism seemed to many observers to have failed its last test of adaptability to the modern world, Yen Fu came along to fill the intellectual void. Beginning in 1898 and continuing for about a decade, translations and summaries of works by Thomas Henry Huxley, Herbert Spencer, John Stuart Mill, Adam Smith, and others flowed from Yen's brush. Yen also added much of his own commentary. Suddenly, within a few years, Chinese intellectuals had within easy reach an immense world of new ideas.

Those new ideas struck China like a thunderclap. The Chinese even began assigning names differently: instead of old standbys like "Admire Mencius," "Virtuous," "Vast Elegance," or "Esteemed Ancestors," names like "Fit" or "Struggle for Existence" were used. The leading reformist newspaper of the time, the name of which might be translated literally as "Current Affairs" or perhaps "The Needs of the Times," came to be known in English as "The Daily Chinese Progress." Coincidentally its editor and leading writer, Liang Ch'i-ch'ao* (1873–1929), was also the man who did most to spread and further Yen Fu's work.

Liang Ch'i-ch'ao and the "New People"   Liang's skills and temperament overlapped with Yen Fu's in ways that made their work complementary. Until he was about twenty-two, Liang's education and contact with Western learning were not unlike Yen's. At the age when Yen went abroad, however, Liang plunged into reform politics, which Yen always avoided. Liang worked closely with K'ang Yu-wei, usually doing newspaper work or teaching. Like K'ang, he had to flee for his life when the Hundred Days reform ended. From then on, Liang's thinking departed from K'ang's and began to develop along more independent lines.

---

* Pronounced *Lee-ong Chee-chow.*

He followed Yen's writing closely and supplemented it with voracious reading in Japan. Liang was deeply impressed by Yen's explanation of struggle, progress, and the importance of individual liberty. He also absorbed Yen's emphasis on the need for changes in men's minds, particularly in the attitudes Chinese held toward social relationships. Yen had reminded his readers of an older saying: "The essence of statecraft is to turn self-interest into public interest." Liang complained that "in China there are duties of individuals to individuals, but there are no duties of individuals to society." Liang set out to do nothing less than transform the Chinese into a "new people." He went at it almost as if he thought he could do it single-handed.

Liang immersed himself in Western writings and flooded one newspaper after another with a torrent of articles in which he translated, summarized, and compared the Greeks, Luther, Bacon, Descartes, Hobbes, Spinoza, Montesquieu, Voltaire, Rousseau, Tolstoy, Kant, Bluntschli, and many others. In a series called "Discourses on the New People," which appeared in the magazine *New People's Fortnightly*, published by Liang in Japan from 1902 to 1907, he also wrote on Cromwell, Napoleon, Bismarck, Mazzini, Garibaldi, and Cavour. A torrent of Western thought, culture, and history poured from his pen to a generation that thirsted for precisely what Liang offered. The series "opened up a new world for me," wrote one of the most famous Chinese intellectuals of the twentieth century, and so it did for thousands.

Liang, elaborating on Yen Fu's work, described a world in which nations and races struggled for existence and only the fit survived; China, to endure, had to renovate its culture. For a time, Liang proposed changes that were thoroughly revolutionary, including the overthrow of the Chinese government. He modified his position between 1903 and 1905, as a result of a trip to the United States and at the urging of K'ang Yu-wei. He no longer called for a revolution, but continued to advocate many social changes and to demand the prompt introduction of genuine constitutional government and a democratic system comparable to England's.

It is not likely that the Chinese court was much influenced by Yen Fu and Liang Ch'i-ch'ao. The court did agree that China should turn to Western models of constitutionalism in order to make her strong enough to throw off Western domination. However, Yen and Liang went further to stress that constitutional and representative government would strengthen the nation by the sharing of power and the participation of the people in politics. Constitutions and parliaments would make it possible to harness to national goals the energies released by clashing opinions. They also emphasized the value of active and direct popular participation in government; they envisioned for China something like the British system, rather than the Japanese or the Prussian. Still, if the area of agreement between the Empress Dowager, Yen, and Liang was smaller than the areas of disagreement, it nevertheless was common ground on which a great many Chinese could meet. Yen and Liang laid the foundations for other conceptions of popular participation and national power.

THE
REVOLU-
TIONARY
MOVEMENT
During the same period in which K'ang Yu-wei, Yen Fu, and Liang Ch'i-ch'ao produced their reform ideas, a more radical current of thought also materialized. Like Yen, Liang, and the Ch'ing court of the 1900s, the radical movement looked to a foreign model of constitutional government, but its inspiration was United States-style republicanism, and its methods were uncompromisingly revolutionary.

Sun Yat-sen (1866–1925), the founder and moving spirit of the revolutionary movement, came to his calling by a peculiarly winding route. His early life was scarcely different from that of tens of thousands of other farmers' sons. But in 1879 Sun joined his older brother in Hawaii. The next fifteen years included education in a British missionary school in Hawaii, a return to his home village during which he offended the villagers by destroying some wooden idols, further British education in Hong Kong culminating in graduation from a medical school, and medical practice in Macao. Throughout the fifteen years Sun's professional education was his major concern, but his interest in social and political problems followed closely behind. He soon abandoned his medical career and spent

the last thirty-one years of his life as a full-time professional revolutionary.

Sun tended to think in terms of contemporary Western
(especially American) standards of nationhood and government. He usually emphasized the need for China to
achieve full national sovereignty, to be independent of all
foreign control, and especially to develop a sense of national community. He was later to stress that the Chinese
people were "scattered sand," granules of families and
clans with no cement of national spirit. Sun's education
and temperament did not equip him to formulate a coherent or profound political philosophy, nor was his career
as a revolutionary conducive to the development of systematic ideas; but to the extent that he was able to think
out a program, it was one of nationalism, democracy, republicanism, and economic modernization.

Nationalism meant to Sun driving out the Manchu rulers
and creating a Chinese-controlled nation-state; democracy
meant a representative system with a strong executive
branch and a system of checks and balances much like
that of the United States; and economic modernization
meant a dimly perceived compromise between socialism and
capitalism that he hoped would avoid the evils of both.
Only to a relatively small extent did he attempt to explain the relevance of his program to Chinese needs and
conditions; Sun's idea for adapting democracy, for example,
was simply to add to the legislative, executive, and judicial
branches two other branches of government that had
functioned in traditional China: One was to administer
the civil service bureaucracy and the other, to be known
as the "control" branch, was intended to inspect the entire
government for signs of malfunctioning.

On the basis of this program Sun regularly appealed to
foreign governments to support his movement, and in his
anxiety to obtain foreign aid he occasionally made rather
extravagant promises of economic concessions in return.
For a long time he remained convinced that the Western
democracies would welcome and help a Chinese democratic
movement. With only a few modifications, his followers,
although resentful of Western imperialism, allowed their

admiration for Western strength and prosperity to out-weigh their resentment.

Sun's ideas were influenced not only by his Western education but also by his early home life and, probably more profoundly, by the overseas Chinese with whom he lived and among whom he traveled for much of his later life. The Chinese in Hawaii, Hong Kong, Japan, Southeast Asia, and all over the world lived in tight communities of their own, islands of industrious immigrants struggling to maintain themselves and at the same time earn something extra to send home. Their settlements remained largely isolated within the countries in which they lived; and without the protection of his family and clan, a Chinese who lived overseas relied on the secret society organizations that had protected commoners in China for centuries. Hence Chinese secret societies, which were essentially mutual aid and mutual protection organizations with mystical-religious ideologies, had active branches in the overseas Chinese communities.

Sun's early revolutionary organizations depended heavily on money contributed by Chinese who lived abroad, especially businessmen. Many of Sun's earliest political associates and most trusted allies were secret society men, often from societies that had branches overseas. His own organizations had initiation rituals, oaths, slogans, sworn brotherhood, and other secret society characteristics. Indeed, one of Sun's recurring problems was that, like a secret society leader, he often insisted on the unquestioning obedience of his followers; he exercised a very personal, cabalistic, almost occult kind of leadership.

Sun's style of leadership found few followers. A poor organizer and an inept tactician, Sun spent an unhappy decade fruitlessly promoting revolution. In the summer of 1905, however, his fortunes changed. And so did the course of modern Chinese history. Sun now became caught up in a swelling tide of revolution that was already changing China more than anyone could see at the time.

Several currents intersected to produce this tide. One was the reform program of the Ch'ing government, which in 1905 not only charted a new political course for China, but also initiated fundamental social changes. Its most important measure was the abolition of the traditional civil service examination system. This measure opened the way for the destruction of the elite group of scholar-gentry, whose social status and privileges had sharply distinguished them from everyone else in China. Similarly, the old educational system, which had been designed to prepare students for the civil service, received a crippling blow, and so did the entire body of Confucian principles that the old education had taught.

The major beneficiaries of these changes were the thousands of students who were sent abroad, mostly to Japan, to receive a new education. From a few hundred in 1902, the number grew to fifteen thousand in 1906. The government hoped they would return to employ their new skills in the service of a modernized Ch'ing state and of the new army it was also attempting to create. But the students, sensitive to the changing intellectual climate in 1901 and 1902, were already listening more to Yen Fu and Liang Ch'i-ch'ao than to the Empress Dowager. When they arrived in Japan the students were dazzled by what they discovered. Japan was on the march. The country bustled with confidence. A militant nationalism spun the wheels of social and economic change, producing goods, weapons, and national pride. Relations with Russia happened to be worsening at the time, and war fever swept the land; when Japan's victory came in 1905, thousands of Chinese students participated vicariously. An Asian nation had demonstrated that it could quickly develop a modern army, navy, economy, and government, and thereby subdue a major Western imperialist power. Reasoning that if Japan could do it, so could China, the students decided that the time had come to dedicate themselves to China's future and to organize for concerted revolutionary action on a large scale.

By 1905 the students' ideas had outraced those of Liang Ch'i-ch'ao, who was lowering his sights precisely when the students were raising theirs. In the absence of other attractive leadership, the students decided to unite behind Sun Yat-sen. But this was not entirely a decision by default. Sun had great personal magnetism, and in ten years of devoted revolutionary work, he had cultivated a wide range of very useful contacts, including secret societies, overseas businessmen, and foreign adventurers and politicians. Some of his exploits had earned him a considerable reputation abroad. A persuasive speaker, he could be useful in future negotiations with the imperialist powers; meanwhile, he could raise money and impress foreigners enough to enhance the reputation of the revolutionary movement. As a medical doctor and at least a nominal Christian, he had qualities no other Chinese leader could match; and there was nothing he wanted more than to overthrow the Ch'ing dynasty and make China a republic, aims that suited the students.

The revolutionary alliance that was forged in the summer of 1905 toiled mightily for six years in behalf of anti-Manchu republicanism, and in that time it grew into a broad coalition of discontented groups. Between October 1911 and February 1912 this rather loose coalition saw its efforts rewarded at last. A revolution overthrew the Ch'ing government and ended the Chinese empire. The alliance between Sun and the students contributed a good deal to the fall of the Ch'ing dynasty and the founding of the Republic of China; most important, it infiltrated the imperial army and weakened the soldiers' will to fight in behalf of the dynasty, and it effectively spread ideas of democracy and republicanism.

Still, the alliance was not solely responsible for the momentous events of 1911 and 1912. Among the several other forces that combined to terminate the ancient imperial system, two must be mentioned here. Ironically both played their roles after being called on stage by the Ch'ing court. The government created the first when, as part of its plan to introduce a limited form of constitutionalism, it decided also to permit elections. Held for the first time in 1909, the elections produced assemblies in each of twenty-one provinces. Few members of the assemblies were revolutionaries, but many were highly critical of the central government, and their vocal demands put added pressure on Peking. Then a national assembly, initiated in 1910, harassed the court still more. But in addition to undermining the authority of the central government, the assemblies provided rallying points for many protesters. Through the assemblies it became possible for landowners, businessmen, educators, journalists, and even some ordinary citizens to become active in politics and to make their voices heard. These people found both their nationalist sensibilities and their economic aspirations outraged by a government railway nationalization plan that favored foreign investors. The assemblies protested but were unheeded, and the members' loyalty to the government evaporated. Thus, new interest groups and new instruments of power, which had been allowed to exist by the Ch'ing court in the hope that they would modernize the government, appease its critics, and strengthen its claim to rule and its ability to enforce that claim, now decided they could better promote their interests by throwing off Ch'ing rule and creating a republic. When the opportunity came in the autumn of 1911, fifteen provincial assemblies declared their independence, and China began to break up into provincial regimes.

In a last-ditch effort to stave off disaster, the Ch'ing court called upon General Yüan Shih-k'ai* (1857–1916), whose help had been decisive in the Empress Dowager's coup of 1898. He had been in retirement since her death in 1908, but his army, which was the best-equipped and best-trained army in China, had remained intact. Yüan negotiated terms with the court that were favorable to himself, entered the fray, fought until a stalemate was created among the revolutionaries, the various provincial regimes, and himself, and then maneuvered adroitly until he managed to obtain the Manchus' abdication. Thus the Ch'ing government committed unintentional suicide by sending students abroad, initiating constitutional and representative government, and inviting back into power the very man who finally forced it to step down.

Yüan Shih-k'ai, by compelling the Manchus to abdicate, persuaded his other rivals for power to accept a compromise. In exchange for ending the empire, he was to become president of the Republic of China, but he in turn was to permit free elections, a parliament, and a system of

---

* Pronounced *Yew-on Shr-kie* (as in "pie").

constitutional government providing for checks and balances and a sharing of power. Sun Yat-sen and his allies accepted a compromise with Yüan because they feared division in the country. Inexperienced, disorganized, woefully lacking in mass support, and afraid that continued disorder might lead the foreign powers to intervene, the republicans chose not to prolong the struggle by military means. They agreed to recognize as president a military man they distrusted and to count on a constitution and their strength in the parliament to control him. Perhaps a bit intoxicated by their own propaganda about the merits of republicanism, they were unduly optimistic that democratic institutions were taking root in China. They lost the gamble. Many of them thereupon renounced political activity in disgust; some even left the country. Speaking for his generation, one émigré explained in a letter to a friend: "Politics is in such confusion that I am at a loss to know what to talk about."

NEW CULTURE AND NATION- ALISM

Governing authority after 1912, and increasingly so between 1916 and 1926, devolved upon "warlords"—military men of narrow vision, limited objectives, and, with few exceptions, mediocre abilities. Each warlord controlled as much territory as he could without taking great risks, taxed as heavily as the people could bear, governed minimally, expanded his army, and maneuvered cautiously to maintain his security vis-à-vis other warlords. All relied heavily on armies whose numbers fluctuated due to the soldiers' unreliability, but which were intended to be personally loyal to an individual warlord. Some had small forces of no more than a few thousand men, but major warlords had armies that occasionally numbered more than a quarter of a million. Some controlled small areas no larger than a county; others controlled several provinces. Some nourished vague ambitions of greater glory, perhaps even a throne; many sought and some obtained aid from foreign powers; a few carried out, usually on a modest scale, social reforms such as attempts to discourage vice or promote education and public works. Some warlords even paid attention to national problems, but for the most part they were concerned only with their own immediate welfare and security.

After the death of Yüan Shih-k'ai in 1916, China had no political leader of national stature; the republic, crippled from the very first, now almost ceased to exist. Its officers and agencies functioned at the whim of whichever warlord managed to hold Peking. That warlord handled China's diplomacy in the name of the republic, but in China his writ extended only to the territory of the neighboring warlord. China was divided among countless satrapies and for a long time after the republican revolution had anything but a modern government. Intellectuals began to think that little had changed despite the fall of the monarchy. They felt that the introduction of reforms over the last fifty years in the armed forces, schools, government, and economy had brought China no closer to being a strong and prosperous nation.

When Japan in 1915 presented to China a set of Twenty-one Demands, the intellectuals' frustration turned to rage. The demands were so far-reaching that it was humiliating merely to be presented with them; only to a country held in utter contempt could Japan have dared to present so naked a claim for virtual colonization. China managed only narrowly to avert full accession to the Japanese demands, and the entire incident provoked immense anger among patriotic Chinese. The day Japan delivered her final ultimatum (May 7) became National Humiliation Day, almost a day of mourning, but also a day of commemoration and rededication. It was in this atmosphere—the failure of republicanism, the renewal of foreign imperialism, and the frustration engendered by failure and weakness—that a handful of Chinese intellectuals undertook to reexamine the problem of modernizing their country.

The intellectuals who surveyed the wreckage of the 1911 revolution were led by men who had not played an important part in it and who felt no stake in justifying it or rationalizing it. They evaluated the revolution coolly and ruthlessly, judging it to have produced a "pseudorepublicanism" under which

we have experienced every kind of suffering known to those who are not free. These sufferings remain the same regardless of political changes or the substitution of one political party in power for another. When politics brings us to such a dead end, we have to arouse ourselves and realize that genuine republicanism can never be achieved until politics is initiated by the people. In order to get the people to initiate politics, we must have as a prerequisite an atmosphere wherein a genuine spirit of free thought and free criticism can be nurtured.

With this ringing denunciation of the republic and call for more popular initiative in politics, China's struggle to modernize entered a new phase. Intellectuals retained continuity with Yen Fu by reaffirming the doctrines of struggle for existence, natural selection, and survival of the fittest, and they demanded a "new culture" much as Liang Ch'i-ch'ao had called for a new people; but the leaders of the New Culture Movement went further than Yen and Liang by condemning all of Chinese tradition. Liang had criticized "those who are infatuated with Western ways and . . . throw away our morals, learning, and customs of several thousand years' standing"; to Ch'en Tu-hsiu* (1879–1942), who by 1915 was on his way to becoming the most influential writer in China, Chinese tradition resided in an antiquated Confucianism that "did not go beyond the privilege and prestige of a few rulers and aristocrats and had nothing to do with the happiness of the great masses." Evaluation of the 1911 revolution led men like Ch'en to conclude that Chinese tradition accounted for the republic's failure. In particular, Confucianism, with its subordination of the young to the old and the individual to the family, stifled the freedom of thought that the people needed in order to bring about true republicanism. Thus New Culture Movement leaders not only continued to uphold ideals of Western democracy and science, but they also promoted those ideals even more fervently and uncompromisingly than earlier modernizing movements; and they went beyond earlier movements in their antitraditionalism and in their appeal for mass participation and even for popular initiative in political action.

---

* Pronounced *Chuhn Doo-shyo.*

In 1915 Ch'en Tu-hsiu founded a magazine called *Youth*, which for the next five years was probably the most widely read and influential publication in China. For the first issue Ch'en wrote a "Call to Youth," in which he urged young people to assume responsibility for eliminating "the old and the rotten" from Chinese life and replacing it with science and democracy. Ch'en's theme was this: "If we expect to establish a Western type of modern nation then the most basic step is to import the foundation of modern Western society—the faith in the equality of men."

Ch'en's "Call to Youth" was heard, and the response was immediate and powerful. Within a few months many of the men who soon dominated Chinese intellectual life were writing tributes to Darwin, the scientific method, the experimental spirit, and liberty, equality and fraternity. Ch'en's magazine changed its name to *The New Youth* and, symbolically, later adopted a French title, *La Jeunesse*. To the English and American influences fostered by Yen Fu, Liang Ch'i-ch'ao, and Sun Yat-sen, China's new youth had added the scientific and French revolutions.

The young people's burgeoning activism was furthered early in 1919 by developments at the Paris Peace Conference. China had entered World War I after much debate. One of the most convincing arguments for participation in the war was that a contribution to victory would entitle China to share in the rewards; the Chinese hoped that at the very least they would regain from the losing powers whatever holdings the losers had in China. Thus the Chinese negotiators at Paris were confident of obtaining the return of Germany's concessions, and, hearing the worldwide proclamations of "territorial integrity" and "national self-determination," they had hopes of obtaining much more. Perhaps even the Twenty-one Demands would be reversed. These hopes were shattered by the revelation at Versailles of secret agreements Japan had made years before with Britain, France, and the warlord government of China. Germany's holdings were not to be returned to China; they had been promised to Japan. Japan's position in China was not to be weakened, but strengthened.

Details of these agreements had trickled into public view during 1918, but at first aroused only small and scattered protests. The protests grew in size and frequency and were supported by new social and economic groups as well as by the intellectuals. The Chinese economy expanded considerably due to the war, and embryonic classes of merchants, industrialists, and workers began to grow. Demonstrations against foreign domination began to bring them into contact with each other and with students and teachers. The minor outbursts of 1918 and early 1919 turned out to be rehearsals for the volcanic political eruption of May 4, 1919.

On May 1 reports from the Chinese delegates revealing that they had lost the diplomatic contest began to appear in the Peking press. Readers were dumbfounded, unbelieving, outraged. Despite all signs to the contrary the public had not been able to believe that the effort to secure China's rights would end in failure. Wilson and others had spoken too well; the world could not ignore the truth and beauty of such noble principles. The disappointment was cataclysmic. One student recalled:

When the news of the Paris Peace Conference finally reached us we were greatly shocked. We at once awoke to the fact that foreign nations were still selfish and militaristic and that they were all great liars. I remember that the night of May 2 very few of us slept. A group of my friends and I talked almost the whole night. We came to the conclusion that a greater world war would be coming sooner or later, and that this great war would be fought in the East. . . . Looking at our people and at the pitiful ignorant masses, we couldn't help but feel that we must struggle!

The struggle burst forth almost at once. The students had planned a demonstration for May 7, National Humiliation Day, but government repression made them decide to move more quickly. Student leaders hurriedly called a meeting for the evening of May 3 and passed a number of resolutions, including one for a mass demonstration the next day. On Sunday morning, May 4, some three thousand students met, drew up manifestos, and marched. Spectators cheered, some wept, and even Western observers were impressed. John Dewey and his wife, who had arrived only a few days earlier to begin a visit that was to last more than two years, wrote home in wonder: "To think of kids in our country from fourteen on, taking the lead in starting a big cleanup reform politics movement and shaming merchants and professional men into joining them. This is sure some country."

As Dewey observantly noted, this was not merely a student demonstration in Peking. It became nationwide, both geographically and socially. A sixteen-year-old high school boy in Ssu-ch'uan, 1,000 miles from Peking, recalled the day he heard the news:

Only a month was left before my graduation. We were having our examination period. And suddenly, like a black Japanese bomb, the Fourth of May exploded over our heads.

Busy with our noisy studying we did not see the teachers running hurriedly to the office of the director. The servants who carried tea to the conference whispered in our inattentive ears: "A letter. . . . Important. From Peking. They don't know whether or not to show the students."

. . . The secretary pasted a long letter on the black announcement board. A thick crowd of students, panting with excitement, gathered quickly around the board. Our best orator, who had a ringing voice and clear enunciation, read every sentence of that remarkable letter. . . .

The letter upset us completely: Boycott . . . Union . . . Constitution . . . Organization . . . Collections . . . All these were strange words. The weight of important political action was laid upon our narrow boyish shoulders.

. . . That night we could not sleep. Our meeting rumbled loudly in the light of oil lamps, and the timid sparrow-like twitter of the younger boys mingled with the harsh breaking voices of the sixteen-year-olds.

. . . Noise, exciting speeches. One student after another came up on the platform. When had they learned to speak? When had they found these ardent gestures—these boys who only yesterday were engaged in childish scuffles. Where did they learn to make those exalted, convincing speeches, to which teachers, directors, and the representatives of merchants now listened so attentively, nodding their heavy heads in time to the angry shouts of their sons and pupils?

The three boys' high schools dedicated themselves, down to the last person, to the anti-Japanese boycott.

. . . Every word of every orator fell into the crackling fire of applause. The treasurer reported the rapid growth of Union funds. I, the secretary, waving over my head a blueprint map of the town, announced how we were going to carry out the boycott.

"All Japanese merchandise must be destroyed," I shouted. "Not a single Japanese object must be hidden. For this, you must elect people whose hands are clean. The Peking comrades summon us to join the strike!"

"The strike!"

The May Fourth incident created an unprecedented wave of patriotism in China. Boycotts, strikes, and demonstrations erupted all over the country and continued for more than a month. Government attempts at repression failed. Rumors circulated that police and soldiers were going to side with the students, merchants, and workers. Several cabinet members resigned. And finally, on June 28, under pressure from Chinese students and workers in France who surrounded its headquarters, the Chinese delegation at Versailles defied its government's instructions and refused to sign the treaty.

But the May Fourth incident was only a partial victory. The secret treaties were not abrogated, and China still had to confront the militant and aggressive Japanese. The confrontation, however, was now on a different basis. The masses were far from mobilized, but nationwide political organization and action had taken place on a scale never before seen in China. A new intelligentsia that had been developing at least since the early 1900s, when thousands of students had gone abroad, had become a major force in Chinese life. Their own organization spanned the country. They had discovered that organized propaganda and demonstrations could bring results. They had tasted the excitement of political activity and some fruits of success. They had made contact with big industrialists and clerks, merchants and laborers, college presidents and janitors, university professors and professional politicians. They had created a pattern for future action and a basis for a new feeling of national commitment, a beginning of a national community and a sense of nationalism. In future confrontations with outside powers China would stand more as a nation than ever before. The combination of freedom and cohesion sought by Yen Fu, the devotion to the public interest called for by Liang Ch'i-ch'ao, the cement of national spirit yearned for by Sun Yat-sen—this common goal of the last twenty years seemed attainable in 1919. The question was whether the new sense of nationhood could be harnessed to the cause of building a new culture. The answer, soon given, was that cultural change was to be subordinated to political action.

KUOMIN-
TANG
REVOLU-
TION
Following the May Fourth Movement, political activists struggled to organize themselves. The only existing party that seemed to offer any immediate promise was the Kuomintang* (KMT), also known as the Nationalist party. Led by Sun Yat-sen, it had grown out of the 1905–1911 revolutionary movement. Since that time Sun had been struggling with only minimal success to keep the party together as a potent political force. From 1920 to 1923 he was nominal head of a nominal KMT government in Canton; in actuality he was little more than an appendage of the local warlord regime, and his position was extremely precarious. Thus he was again looking for firmer sources of support precisely at a time when many Chinese were bent on political action; KMT ranks began to grow accordingly.

Sun, as usual, was anxious for foreign help. It turned out that the only place from which help was forthcoming was the Soviet Union. At the same time, Chinese intellectuals were also beginning to pay closer attention to the Soviet Union. Their interest in Russia, which had grown slowly after the Bolshevik Revolution of 1917, snowballed in the post-May Fourth atmosphere. The Bolsheviks helped to encourage this interest (with policies we shall explain later), but equally important encouragement came inad-

* Pronounced *Gwaw-min-dong*.

vertently from the West and Japan. The imperialist powers had already alienated the Chinese at Versailles. Then they created a bond of sympathy between China and Russia by invading Russia and supporting anti-Bolshevik forces and regimes. As the West turned its demonic side to China once again, Chinese ambivalence shifted away from its admiration for Western-style democracy and toward anti-imperialism. The availability of an alternate foreign model doubtless facilitated the renewal of Chinese anti-Westernism. Scores of Soviet-oriented groups of many kinds sprouted in 1920 and 1921. In July 1921 the Chinese Communist Party (CCP) was formally organized, and Ch'en Tu-hsiu became its head. In 1923, thanks to the tireless efforts and adroit maneuvering of the Soviet Union, a KMT-CCP united front was set up.

The Emergence of a New Kuomintang, 1923–1924   Like the Communists, the Kuomintang entered upon the united front because its leaders thought the benefits it would bring in the short run outweighed the long-run risks. Indeed, the appeal of a united front to both sides was precisely that both were concerned chiefly with immediate problems and only marginally with future ones. Most of all, the leaders of both the KMT and the CCP came to the conclusion that their movements were stymied unless they could mobilize enough power to eliminate the warlords and take a strong stand against Western and Japanese imperialism. Each was too weak to do this alone, and so they were logical allies.

The KMT had several more specific reasons for agreeing to collaborate with the CCP. After nearly thirty years of unstinting effort, Sun Yat-sen had obtained only sporadic and sparing foreign help. He had scarce financial reserves and no reliable sources of funds. He had built no effective party organization. The party, in addition to being loosely organized, had a small membership that was not broadly representative of Chinese society. Among its most numerous and influential members were intellectuals whose education was obtained mostly overseas, businessmen whose orientation was toward Western commerce, and Chinese scattered over numerous overseas communities. Many KMT leaders, and most of all Sun, believed that with the help of the Soviet Union and the CCP their party could strengthen its organization and broaden its membership.

Sun Yat-sen was therefore highly receptive to overtures made by the Soviet Union in 1922. After negotiations lasting into the next year, a declaration was issued jointly by Sun and a Soviet emissary named Adolf Joffe. In a statement that he soon qualified, Sun stipulated, "the Communistic order or even the Soviet system cannot actually be introduced into China, because there do not exist here the conditions for the successful establishment of either Communism or Sovietism." Joffe added: "China's paramount and most pressing problem is to achieve national unification and attain full national independence"; to these ends Joffe promised Russian "sympathy" and "support." The most concrete evidence of Russian sympathy and support was the arrival in China of advisers, money, and weapons. All three began pouring in after further discussions, some of which were held in the Soviet Union between Russian leaders and a Chinese delegation headed by Chiang Kai-shek* (1887———).

Sun Yat-sen had meanwhile to counter doubts in his own sharply divided party. In its influential right wing were many who questioned the wisdom of accepting Soviet support and cooperating with the Chinese Communists. There was great concern about the possibility of excessive Russian influence, and there was fear that the Communists would prove to be unreliable and excessively radical allies. The vigor with which Sun attempted to persuade his followers suggests that the opposition among them was great. It was finally agreed that the Communists would be allowed to join the KMT but could retain their own separate party. Many of Sun's followers remained disturbed about the dangers of subversion, and they were only partly reassured when Sun bluntly told the Soviet emissary that the Communists "must submit to discipline and not criticize the Kuomintang openly. If the Communists do not submit to the Kuomintang, I shall expel them; and if Soviet Russia should give them secret protection, I shall

---

* Pronounced *Jee-ong Kye* (as in "rye") -*shek*.

oppose Soviet Russia." Sun also tried to persuade his followers that they needed outside help and could obtain it nowhere else, that the Chinese Communists were too small and weak a group to carry out a revolution, that the Russians had no choice but to work with the KMT if they wanted to "collaborate with China," and most of all that the outlook, needs, and interests of the Russians and the KMT coincided.

Sun invoked both ideology and tactical considerations to justify his policy. On the one hand, Sun argued that communist doctrine was not significantly different from his own Three People's Principles of nationalism, democracy, and people's livelihood. His last two principles were less congruent with Soviet doctrine than nationalism was, but, in Sun's opinion, the gap had been narrowed ever since the Soviet Union had adopted the New Economic Policy. Furthermore, Sun held, the Russians were increasingly emphasizing nationalism, where their agreement with the Chinese was greatest. Sun insisted that too many of his followers were exaggerating the ideological differences between the KMT and the Soviet Union.

Sun also took pains to explain how the Russians' experience could be immensely valuable in curing what had been the KMT's most persistent ailment: its inability to become a popular mass movement. In December 1923 the Soviet foreign minister wrote to Sun that propaganda and organization were the first necessities in building a powerful movement. He added: "Our example was significant: our military activities were successful because a long series of years had elapsed during which we organized and instructed our following, building up in this way a great organized party throughout the whole land, a party capable of vanquishing all its adversaries." Virtually as this letter was being written, Sun was telling a party meeting that the party had relied too heavily upon military force.

What was the power that we lacked? It was the support of the people. . . .

. . . Why has not our Party engaged in organized, systematic, and disciplined struggle before? It was because we lacked the model and the precedent. . . . If we wish our revolution to succeed, we must learn the methods, organization, and training of the Russians; then there can be hope of success. . . . The reason behind the Communist Party's success is that it suits the desires of the majority of the Russian people, so all the Russian people support it.

Sun immediately launched a sustained effort to spell out his own ideas. In a series of sixteen lectures to top party representatives between January and August 1924, Sun developed anew his Three People's Principles and gave them significantly new emphases. His principle of nationalism now stressed anti-imperialism in a way that fitted the new pro-Soviet orientation of his party; his principle of democracy stressed more than ever before the weaknesses of representative systems and the need for strong government; and his principle of people's livelihood attached a new importance to its similarity to socialism and its opposition to capitalism. Furthermore, while Sun spelled out his ideas, the manifesto of the first Kuomintang Party Congress stressed the importance of party power, party centralization, and the mobilization of the masses for action.

The pillars of KMT policy came to be admission of the Communists into the KMT, alliance with the Soviet Union, creation of a party army, and mobilization of the masses of workers and peasants. With Russian guidance and financial backing and Chinese Communist assistance in organization and propaganda, the KMT became a more disciplined, Communist-style party with growing support among the masses and the nucleus of a party army.

THE RISE OF CHIANG KAI-SHEK
The leader of the new KMT army, Chiang Kai-shek, was among those followers of Sun who remained unreconciled to the reorientation of the party. As late as 1926, however, Chiang was supporting the united front enough to ask an American reporter indignantly, "Why does she [the United States] preach fine sermons, but in the end tag along with the others [imperialist powers]? Why does she not, like Russia, prove her friendliness by acts?" (Questions such as these earned for Chiang the now ludicrous sobriquet "Red general.") But he soon struck fiercely at the Communists

and reoriented once again the Kuomintang and the Chinese revolution.

After a visit to the Soviet Union Chiang recalled:

From my observations and from my conversations I became convinced that Soviet political institutions were instruments of tyranny and terror, and basically incompatible with the Kuomintang's political ideals. . . . I came to the conclusion that the possibility of a revival of Czarist ambitions against China could not be ruled out. . . . I felt strongly that Russia's stratagem and program of World Revolution could constitute an even greater menace to our national independence than had Western colonialism.

Chiang relates that he served Sun in the united front because Sun appealed so persuasively to his party loyalty. But Sun Yat-sen died in March 1925; maneuvering for leadership in the party began soon thereafter.

Within a year after Sun's death, Chiang had gone far toward resolving the succession crisis and consolidating his leadership in the party. In March 1926 he felt strong enough to move against the Communists. By a series of bold political and military strokes, Chiang reduced the power of Russian and Chinese Communists in the KMT, strengthened his own position in the party and as commander-in-chief of the National Revolutionary Army, and launched the Northern Expedition. His armies swept rapidly over much of southeast China; by March 1927 Chiang had established a new base for the KMT in the lower Yangtze* River valley, anchored in Shanghai and in Nanking, which became the KMT capital. A month later he moved against the Communists again, this time even more boldly, decisively, and viciously than in 1926; now the Communists were not merely checked, but crushed.

Chiang Kai-shek's victories over the Communists did not place him in an entirely secure position. There were other old enemies yet to be confronted, particularly some of the major warlords; there was also Japan, which

---

* Pronounced *Yong-dzuh.*

watched with growing anxiety the rise of a new nationalistic movement backed by a substantial army. Even in his own party, moreover, Chiang had exacerbated old tensions and created new ones, especially among those who opposed abrogating Sun's united front policy so summarily. These problems continued to plague Chiang and the government he founded in 1928. Most of all, Japan's anxiety grew quickly into outright military aggression; and by the time it did, the Communists were reorganizing themselves and beginning to worry Chiang.

In brief, Chiang Kai-shek's rise was rapid, but his power was severely limited. Nevertheless, the KMT had been transformed, and its position in the country had changed radically between 1923 and 1928. Instead of its narrow and shaky base in Canton, the KMT now controlled most of two provinces in the lower Yangtze area and substantial parts of several other provinces; it possessed the most powerful single military force in China; it had become a better organized and more disciplined party; it had broadened its support by making inroads into the laboring classes, rural as well as urban; and it had produced a daring and decisive new leader. With considerable help from the Soviet Union and the Chinese Communists, the KMT had done more to unify the country than any leaders for at least sixty years, thereby earning more respect from the foreign powers than China had received within anyone's memory. A strong, united, and prosperous China was not yet around the corner, but in 1928 there was hope again.

*　　　*　　　*

At the beginning of the twentieth century China's leaders had chosen to begin systematically to import foreign ideas and institutions. The imports came in rapid succession from Prussia and Japan, England and the United States, the France of Robespierre and Danton, the Russia of Lenin, and scientists and philosophers the world over. In 1928, with the prospects for effective government better than they had been for many years, the time had come to see whether the new ideas and practices could help solve problems that had long been neglected.

In the thirty years that preceded the founding of the Kuomintang government, China had experienced an intellectual revolution of massive proportions. Education had been transformed, and the old scholar-bureaucrats had been replaced by a new intellectual elite. The new intelligentsia was militantly antitraditional, increasingly radical, and inclined primarily toward Marxist and positivist assumptions and values; but it was still a far from unified group of people. Intellectuals could come closest to unanimity when they discussed the scientific method, the epistemology of science, the inevitability of some form of socialism, and the need for industrialization, all of which were widely accepted. All else was ruthlessly questioned, and a lively diversity made the air crackle with ideas. In universities and new research organizations intellectuals pursued their work with imagination and fervor. In the realm of ideas China's revolution proceeded apace.

In the same period changes also touched other parts of Chinese society, but not as deeply or widely. Industry and trade began to grow, the traditional family system began to break down, women gained considerable independence, and business and labor classes expanded and organized. But the growth of new ideas far outstripped social changes, and in the countryside the lag was greater still. In the major cities a few thousand intellectuals were discussing in sophisticated terms the ideas of the world's greatest thinkers; elsewhere, old beliefs and an antiquated institutional structure held sway over the lives of 500 million people. The new ideas had to be translated into solutions for problems of hunger, disease, overpopulation, and underproduction, and political life had to be fundamentally reorganized at the same time. China once again arrived at a fork in the road. A "new culture" had to be broadened beyond a small urban intellectual elite.

Chapter 3

Modernization under the Kuomintang Government 1928-1949

The Nationalist government still survives on Taiwan; however, it is generally recognized to have been the official government of China only from 1928 to 1949. During the entire twenty years of KMT rule, hardly a day passed that a frightful number of Chinese did not die in civil war or in fighting against Japan. Against these conditions of prolonged strife, the hopes of 1928 were dashed.

From 1928 to 1937 the Kuomintang government had its best opportunity to function. Although its authority extended to only a fraction of China's area (and even in that fraction its rule was not unchallenged), the KMT had momentum and considerable popular support, and it could call upon a substantial pool of administrative and technical talent. Even though that pool was much too shallow to supply all the country's needs, the party was able to make a start toward solving some major problems.

From 1937 to 1945 China was at war with Japan. For a young government, newly emerging from decades of foreign oppression and internal disorder, the demands of a prolonged war against a major mechanized military power were excessive. The war brought to the Chinese people destruction, deprivation, and suffering that can scarcely be imagined. Casualties among Chinese regular troops are estimated at 10 million; there were at least another 3.5 million dead, wounded, and injured among guerrilla troops, militia, and civilians. One hint of the human cost is the fact that between 1938 and 1944 nearly 50 million refugees are said to have received relief aid. Since we may be sure that at least an equal number went unaided, it would be conservative to guess that 100 million human lives were shattered by the war. Suffering on so gigantic a scale, enough in itself to demoralize a society, created huge problems for the government, which were aggravated because the Japanese invasion forced it to move inland from the coastal areas and abandon the most highly developed sectors of the country. Such harsh circumstances have led many scholars to conclude that it was above all the accidents of war that caused the KMT to be defeated.

Compelling though this argument is, it may also be said that the KMT did not make the most of the opportunities it had. In 1928 the KMT controlled only a small area in parts of Che-chiang and Chiang-su. By about 1934 it controlled most of those two provinces, at least four others, and parts of three more; it also had considerable influence in six additional provinces. Pursuit of the Communists in 1934 and 1935 extended KMT power to at least four other provinces, and during the war three more moved closer to the KMT government. The outbreak of war with Japan in 1937 produced a new surge of patriotism, of which Chiang Kai-shek was the major symbol, and the country closed ranks as it had not done at least since 1919. Even the Communists, who had an opportunity to eliminate him at the end of 1936, were forced to admit that Chiang offered China her best chance for unity, and indeed perhaps her only chance at that time. Thus the war was not entirely without its positive side for KMT rule and Chiang Kai-shek's personal leadership. The challenge was to convert such opportunity into a reality that could withstand the arduous tests of the 1940s. The KMT was unable to build upon the unity of 1937, however, and by the end of the war Chiang was no longer the country's unquestioned leader. Instead of being in a position where he could claim to have led the nation successfully through one of the greatest crises it had ever faced, Chiang found that his government had lost ground to the Communists. Although the KMT had been at least the nominal leader of the wartime resistance, in 1945 the CCP controlled about one-fifth of the country and was prepared to challenge the KMT for control of the rest.

In the last period of Chiang's rule on the mainland, following a brief effort (under United States pressure) to negotiate a settlement in 1945 and 1946, the Kuomintang and Communists fought a civil war. As long as the Nationalist government exists on Taiwan, the civil war cannot be considered to have ended formally, but for most practical purposes its outcome was decided by the end of 1948. Offensives in Manchuria in May and June 1947 turned the military tide in favor of the Communists; support for the Kuomintang, waning steadily for some years, was almost totally eliminated because of Chiang's political, economic, and military blunders. In 1949 Chiang, his government, and his army fled to Taiwan. The Communists founded a new government in Peking, and in their turn confronted problems very similar to those the KMT had faced. The two governments' approaches to those problems show faint parallels but glaring contrasts.

POLITICAL UNITY   Early twentieth-century revolutionaries thought that republicanism and constitutional government provided relatively simple and very nearly complete answers to China's political problems. The Kuomintang inherited this spirit of uncritical imitation of Western political institutions; when Sun Yat-sen became more critical of the West, his party followed his example. This change of policy created an ambivalence that the KMT was never able to resolve.

Sun had never been an entirely uncritical admirer of the West, but his praise of Western institutions, his belief in the need for Western aid, and his confidence in the value of Western models for a long time outweighed his occasional reservations. He had been the earliest and most insistent advocate of United States-style republicanism, but after 1911 he began to criticize the opportunities it offered for what he called a "congressional absolutism" that weakened the authority of the executive branch, and he objected to the federal principle insofar as it contributed to disunity. Eventually he came around to a position resembling that of the nineteenth-century reformers.

As soon as we learn Western machinery we can use it anytime, anywhere. . . . But Western social customs and sentiments are different from ours in innumerable points; . . . Hence this difference: in ways of controlling physical objects and forces we should learn from the West, but in ways of controlling men, we should not learn only from the West.

The last part of Sun's statement still assigned to Western models a partial role in guiding Chinese social change, but it also opened up the possibility of a compromise with tradition, which the KMT was soon to pursue further. This compromise took the form of the five-power constitution Sun had been calling for since about 1905. In this scheme, the executive, legislative, and judicial branches known in the West would be supplemented by the civil service and control powers taken from traditional China. Sun regarded his conception of constitutional government as "a new discovery" in political theory and "a fundamental solution" to the problem of establishing democracy in China.

Sun claimed that his solution would give the government enough power to govern and yet enable the people to control their government as efficiently as they could turn on a water faucet or flick an electric switch. (Sun's choice of metaphor is typical of his propensity to think in Western terms, and it also reveals his tendency to view government as a machine or gadget.) "We who have vision and foresight," Sun said, would first build an "all-powerful" government administrative machinery based upon the five-power constitution. The five administrative powers would be controlled by four "political powers" held by the people—suffrage, recall, initiative, and referendum. "Then we will have a completely democratic government organ, and the strength of the people and of the government will be well balanced. . . . With these nine powers in operation and preserving a balance, the problem of democracy will truly be solved and the government will have a definite course to follow."

To bring constitutional government into existence, Sun provided for a revolution in three stages. In 1905 he had prescribed that the first step would be unification of the country by military action; then a military government would rule for about three years. As old evils were eradicated and order restored, military law would be replaced by local self-government under a provisional constitution. Sun believed that, because the Chinese people were politically inert, they needed a gradual initiation into democracy; a period of tutelage was required as an interim step. This stage would last about six years, after which there would be a final stage in which military government and tutelage would be eliminated and full constitutional government introduced. This formulation was later modified a good deal, but the basic idea of three stages remained; the most important modification, clearly stated in the 1914 regulations of the KMT, was the proviso that in the period between the outbreak of military action and the promulgation of the constitution the responsibility for all policy would be borne by the party. For the first time the concept of party tutelage was explicitly enunciated. By 1924 Sun was urging that China follow the Russian example of "placing the party above the state." The idea of party tutelage was a natural corollary to his concept that certain people (of whom Sun was one) "have vision and foresight" and that it is they who should have responsibility for building the machinery of the state. Sun was a highly inconsistent thinker, and he did not hold steadily to the idea of party tutelage; it was, however, one of his more important ideas, and it became a pillar of KMT policy.

When the KMT turned to the task of political unification in 1928, it enshrined Sun's ideas as holy writ, above criticism; an almost mystical cult of Sun was fostered. But in more mundane practice too the government followed much of Sun's blueprint. Even as early as 1925, less than four months after Sun died and a full year before the

Northern Expedition carried the party's flag out of Canton, the KMT Central Executive Committee had promulgated a law that provided for party direction of national affairs. In 1928, virtually simultaneous with the conclusion of the Northern Expedition, the party proclaimed the beginning of tutelage and the establishment of a five-branch structure of government corresponding to Sun's ideas of a five-power constitution. In subsequent years the party spent much of its time either debating the nature and duration of tutelage and the propriety of having a constitution during the tutelage period or writing constitutions and other legal documents. There was a constant tinkering with one or another foreign-style mechanism or device. The party's preoccupation with such matters is symptomatic of its failure to come to grips with the central problems of political unification.

An elaborate traditional administrative system had been shattered by more than a century of dynastic decline, revolution, and foreign wars; decades of social change and political experimentation had further eroded the old system. This erosion had permitted the development of even more local autonomy and administrative variations than had been customary. Thus the fundamental political problems centered on how to integrate a changing polity that included old-fashioned warlord satrapies, new parties and independent political clubs, modern and traditional political interest groups, and a vast range in between. Furthermore, political integration had to be attempted in the face of armed challenges from the Chinese Communists, Russia, and Japan, and amid a host of other foreign pressures.

The party's solutions to these problems were shaped by its own history at least as much as they were by Sun Yat-sen's ideas. Its revolutionary heritage was not suddenly erased when the party came to power. But during the 1920s membership multiplied many times, and the party came to be led by military and merchant groups. Many of its leaders had been educated abroad, especially in Japan, the United States, and Western Europe, and they came from the coastal areas of China that had been most exposed to treaty-port influence. The result was that policies were reversed in rapid succession. The military, for example, which had been built along Soviet lines, now hired German advisers and adopted a system modeled on Germany and Japan. China's models remained foreign and modern, but they now came from the political right instead of the left.

The sudden growth of the party, coinciding with the acquisition of power, created new internal stresses and aggravated old ones. Competition for the fruits of victory split the KMT into many factions, and Chiang Kai-shek had to maneuver adroitly to consolidate his leadership. Divisions within the party demanded so much of the leadership's attention that little time was available for dealing with the country's problems. More important, almost every decision required a massive effort at coalition-building. The resulting policies rested on flimsy ad hoc agreements, and the policy makers became laden with a double burden—political debts to their allies and the enmity of those they had outmaneuvered.

Alliances among party factions, warlords, and other groups shifted bewilderingly, and the maneuverings continued for years. While jousting of this sort prevailed at the level of national politics, the problem of local administration festered. Vast areas of the country lay beyond the Kuomintang's reach. Tens of millions of people neither contributed taxes needed by the government nor received the services they needed in order to improve their lives and feel that they were citizens of a nation. The faction-ridden government attempted to concentrate power in its own hands. Strict surveillance of local authorities by the provincial government and provincial authorities by the central government thwarted local officials. They lacked autonomy and training needed to adapt general policies to varying local conditions; at the same time the central government failed to supplement its general directives with special instructions for particular localities. As a torrent of legislation, procedural rules, governing principles, administrative regulations, and action programs poured out of Nanking, a huge but top-heavy apparatus of party and government workers struggled to implement them.

The laws and action programs were often reasonably well designed by knowledgeable political practitioners and theorists, and party and government workers were frequently educated, experienced, and dedicated men. But the designers, especially the large proportion who had been educated abroad and returned to live in the large modernizing cities like Shanghai, could not take into account the diverse problems of 1,500 to 2,000 far-flung districts; and the *hsien* staffs were too small (the average size was about eighty people who governed an area and population about the size of Delaware) and generally not familiar with the details of their districts to adapt the directives from the central government to local circumstances, even when they had the will and motivation. There were too many programs on paper that had little relationship to what the population needed and wanted, and the men charged with the awesome burden of translating directives into action hardly knew where to begin. Government and party offices, mapped out neatly on rational organization charts as befits a modern state and political party, failed to carry out their functions at the local level.

In the *hsien* capital, a government-appointed magistrate and his small staff tried to deal with the crucial day-to-day problems that touched people's lives most directly—land administration, education, elections, public works, tax collection, health and sanitation, relief, law enforcement, military conscription. The magistrate had to produce the results that Nanking wanted, and since he could not do everything he had to assign priorities according to those of the central government. Those priorities stressed tax collection, police work, and conscription. One *hsien,* for example, allotted approximately 90 percent of its budget for salaries paid to administrative officials. But so few resources went into education, welfare, and development projects that only about 30 percent of the school-age children attended school, and the administration of the government's model land reform law remained so underdeveloped that the entire *hsien* Department of Land Administration was finally abolished and replaced by two officials. Without land reform and educational opportunities, farmers remained poor and their children remained uneducated.

The problem of political unity remained unsolved. Twenty years after its founding, Chiang Kai-shek's political apparatus had still failed to unite the people. In 1948 a Ssu-ch'uan farmer named Lin, living about 50 miles from his *hsien* capital, which in turn was about 12 miles from China's wartime national capital of Chungking, commented that he had heard of the Kuomintang but had never had any personal contact with it. The government had placed Lin and his family in a group with thirteen other families, who were convened for a meeting whenever instructions had to be passed along. Instructions filtered down intermittently through several tiers before reaching the fourteen families. These tiers were the heart of the relatively informal apparatus through which the government attempted to supplement its more formal government and party structure.

The group of fourteen families made up a ward; together with nine other wards of approximately the same size (a total of 150 families, about 850 people, living in an area roughly a mile square), it belonged to an administrative unit called a borough; thirty-one boroughs made up a township, and seventy-one townships a *hsien*. Through these tiers the *hsien* administration attempted to govern the 800,000 people in its district. Heads of families constituted a ward assembly, which was to elect a borough assembly, which in turn would elect the township assembly, which was to elect a *hsien* political council. According to theory, this system was to result eventually in the end of KMT one-party tutelage and its replacement by free popular exercise of the rights of suffrage, recall, initiative, and referendum. Theory, in other words, called for a thoroughly democratic process of local self-government. But elections for borough and township assemblies and for the *hsien* political council only formalized, institutionalized, and perpetuated the power that wealthy men had exercised for generations over men like farmer Lin. "There isn't a single tenant in the whole Council," observed a high *hsien* official in 1948. "Many of the Council members are able men, but they are all men of wealth, education, and leisure. They are conservative and aren't interested in changing the *status quo*. The *status quo* is not bad at all from their own personal point of view, which is the only point of view most of them have."

SOCIAL AND
CULTURAL
CHANGE

Political integration was inseparable from social problems. Class consciousness and differing living styles, attitudes, and customs divided not only the wealthy and educated from the poor and illiterate, but also the modern-educated from the traditionally educated and the city poor from the rural poor. Divisions cut many other ways as well. A single family might include illiterate peasant parents, a son who was a struggling urban worker, a son who was a returned student from America (and perhaps a Christian) and employed by a Western firm in Shanghai, and a daughter who insisted on choosing her own husband.

Of the many divisive stresses felt by individuals and families, two have particularly troubled political leaders in modern China. One has been the conflict between loyalty to the family and loyalty to the nation; the other has been the clash between traditional culture and modern culture, accentuated by the prevalent belief that change from traditional to modern could only occur if it were also change from Chinese to Western: To modernize was to Westernize and therefore to cut off one's cultural roots. This was liberating and therefore satisfying, but it also left an aftertaste of guilt. Young Chinese, still sensitive to their deep tradition and lengthy history, felt a disquieting suspicion that the uprooting might have been premature and therefore a form of cultural murder. As one writer put it, China had come to "worship all foreigners" and had become their pupil; "the result is material improvement, but spiritual degeneration." Many felt alone and adrift on a foreign sea.

As antiforeign patriotism swept the country, the intellectuals who had taken the lead in the Westernization movement of the early twentieth century felt guilty at having rejected their ancestors in favor of foreign ways. Many of them took refuge in nationalist movements as a way of resolving their internal conflicts; rejection of their families could be justified in the name of loyalty to the nation, and Westernization could be explained as a movement to establish the universal values of equality and justice and to build a greater China. Thus nationalism seemed capable of resolving both major conflicts by placing nation above family and by concurrently serving to replace the old cultural tradition with something else that was distinctively Chinese—the nation.

The masses were affected differently, although no less seriously. We know less about what happened to so-called ordinary people, but we do know that the impact of Western ideas faded quickly as it passed beyond the walls of major cities. Vast areas of the country were hardly touched by changes such as the rise of nationalism. Early in 1936 patriotic students marched into villages near Peking and attempted to arouse the peasants against Japanese invaders who were virtually at the villagers' doorstep. One farmer's response was typical: "The present governor seems all right. Our taxes are lower than before. Why bother us?" Further inland, William Hinton has reported, peasants were even more isolated but so wretchedly preoccupied with survival that they resembled men standing in a well up to their necks in water—the slightest ripple would be enough to drown them, and yet they could no more envision new possibilities than they could survey the sky.

For political leaders seeking to reintegrate the society and mobilize its resources, this many-faceted and amorphous cultural crisis posed a variety of concrete challenges. One of the most persistent was to bridge the widening gap between the city and the countryside. Life in major cities was turning toward Western styles and becoming dominated by businessmen, intellectuals, politicians, and soldiers who looked to the West. Foreign enclaves, having been regarded in the nineteenth century primarily as centers of foreign pollution, had become in the twentieth century not only objects of anti-imperialist agitation, but also havens for revolutionaries and examples of new ways of living. Shanghai, Nanking, and other large cities contained only a small proportion of China's half-billion people, but at least 15 million people lived in the twelve largest cities and many more millions lived in sizable cities. China's urban inhabitants were numerous, potentially influential, and coming to believe in the possibility of a very different life than their fathers had known.

In the countryside, by contrast, changes were only beginning to touch a handful of wealthy people, some of whom served in the new organs of local government or received some modern education. Three-quarters or more of the parents continued to arrange their children's marriages, and three-quarters or more of the children continued to consider it their highest duty to follow their parents' wishes; three-quarters or more of the people continued to conceive of life as offering the same possibilities it had offered to their fathers and grandfathers.

To those who saw the new possibilities, a Western education was becoming the surest route to status, influence, and prosperity, especially in the fields of government service, business, and the professions. The opportunity to be educated abroad, however, came no more easily to the poor under the republic than it had before. While the number of Chinese students increased markedly, the proportion of those who received government support dipped; thus students going abroad had to support themselves, and few besides the wealthy urbanites could do so.

The Kuomintang government was unable to solve this problem. It could not sufficiently extend and improve Chinese education; it could not make foreign education more widely available; and it could not free itself from relying heavily upon men who had Western training. Indeed, between 1932 and 1947, perhaps as many as 70 or 80 percent of high government officials were men who had been educated abroad. This was not necessarily harmful, but it turned out to have some baleful effects on Chinese modernization. A United States mining engineer, working in China as an adviser on mineral resources in the early 1940s, complained that all the Western-trained geologists he met excelled at making maps and charts, but would not dirty their hands in the field. He claimed that none of them had discovered a single mineral deposit and that all the mines and oil and salt wells he visited had been worked by local peasants for centuries. His comment may have been somewhat unfair, but in general it cannot be said that the Western-educated elite dug their hands very deeply into the morass of China's needs. Many, for example, studied agricultural subjects abroad but returned to teach Western-style scientific agriculture in college or work in other occupations; their prescriptions for rural China slighted problems such as high rents, insecurity, usury, and absentee landlordism. Many returned engineers worked for foreign firms in large cities and contributed little to Chinese development. A high proportion of business students returned to work in Western or Western-style banks in large cities. Of the many who returned to China to take up teaching careers, most did so at the highest levels of education, which also kept them in the larger cities.

In short, modern education deepened the gulf between city and country, between educated elite and uneducated masses, and between those oriented toward Western life and those oriented toward traditional Chinese life. The KMT did not create this situation, but once in power the party perpetuated and even worsened it. The modern elite, now rapidly increasing in numbers, staffed the new universities, banks, trading companies, and the party and government bureaucracies, but their training did not equip them to deal with the problems that lay beyond the city walls. They expanded the system of higher education, managed the growing trade, worked wonders in currency reform, restructured the party and the government, and improved services such as the postal and transportation networks. Meanwhile, remnants of the old elite, whose forebears had bitterly resisted modernization in the nineteenth century but accepted limited constitutionalism in the twentieth, continued to dominate the countryside from small villages right up to the *hsien* level.

The KMT allowed several experiments in rural reconstruction that revealed both the potential power of innovation and some of the pitfalls. Its own Rural Service sent students to the countryside during their vacations, but this was more a strictly limited economic effort to help bring in the harvest than it was an attempt to bridge the gap between urban and rural society. Perhaps the most famous experiment was the Mass Education Movement directed by James Y. C. Yen (Yen Yang-ch'u). Educated at Yale and Princeton, Yen had worked with the Chinese Labor Corps in France during World War I and had developed a system for quickly teaching basic literacy. In 1930, with financial support from American missionaries and the backing of local leaders and the Nanking government, Yen launched a pilot project in a northern *hsien*. The project was aimed at a wide range of rural needs, including improved agricultural production and sanitation, but it began with an attempt to wipe out illiteracy in the hope that other problems could then be solved primarily by means of education. Yen also believed in starting at the village level and working up to the *hsien*.

The program was successful enough to warrant further experimentation along the same lines. But of greater interest than a balance sheet of success or failure is Yen's estimate of the obstacles to social change and their historical background. Reflecting on how matters stood in rural reconstruction in 1937, he discerned a historical pattern into which his movement and others of the 1930s fit. Two movements that had been essentially destructive and had relied primarily on force of arms (the T'ai-p'ing Rebellion in the nineteenth century and the 1911 revolution) had each been followed by a movement that was more constructive and peaceful (the T'ai-p'ings by late nineteenth-century reforms such as those of 1898, and 1911 by the May Fourth Movement). These constructive movements, he implied, had not touched the rural masses. Now the revolution of 1926 was being followed by rural reconstruction. History had at last produced a national and cultural "self-awareness" that had in turn promoted rural reform.

Yen's approach to rural change resembled much of what the Communists later said and did. He wrote: "In the solution of rural problems, the first thing is to rely on rural people as the main force; secondly, it is also necessary to rely on people who have knowledge, vision, new methods and new techniques (which rural people do not have) to unite with them." In the preceding ten years, Yen found, this dawning awareness of common purpose was reflected in the intellectuals' slogan Go to the people. He continued: "Formerly, educated Chinese only read books and wrote essays; they left practical work to farmers, artisans, and merchants. But today's intellectuals realize that if learning is not related to real life it is bound to be empty and sterile." The task was now to work from the roots outward, as he had tried to do in his pilot project, and this could be done only if intellectuals "went down to the countryside" (*hsia-hsiang*) and if the worlds of politics and learning intermingled. In his model *hsien,* all had, he said, "realized the need to make scholarship politicized and to have politics become scholarly." Elsewhere he spoke of "the unity of politics and study."

Yen's experiment suffered from weaknesses that included excessive paperwork and top-heavy structure. Nevertheless, it showed that Western-educated Chinese could dedicate themselves to solving the elemental problems faced by the millions in the countryside. James Yen's experiment was not a panacea, and it was not the only experiment; there were others that resembled his in the rural areas, still others in small urban communities, and yet others that concentrated on vocational education or emphasized something other than education. But the government provided only marginal support for all of them.

Chiang Kai-shek had his own ideas about social change, and, to the relatively limited extent that the Kuomintang government engaged in social reform at all, it followed Chiang's ideas. He believed that the Confucian virtues should be rejuvenated and made the basis of modern reforms. This approach to social change was embodied in the New Life Movement, which he initiated with a speech in Chiang-hsi in February 1934. The time and place suggest that Chiang's interest in social reform had immediate and specific political ramifications that in his mind outweighed social reform as a worthy goal in itself. Chiang's speech came in the midst of his fifth massive campaign to smash the Communist forces that had settled in Chianghsi; Nanchang, which was headquarters for the campaigns, also housed the Central Association of the New Life Movement and was the site of its various model projects. Not until about a year after the Communists abandoned Chiang-hsi and marched north was the Central Association transferred to Nanking.

The New Life Movement functioned quite differently in Chiang-hsi than it did elsewhere. In Chiang-hsi it was designed to gain popular support in the struggle against the Communists and to win back for the Kuomintang the loyalty of those who had lived under the Chinese soviet regime. Thus the KMT actively promoted the New Life Movement in the Chiang-hsi countryside, where it was aimed chiefly at physical rehabilitation of recaptured areas. Elsewhere the New Life Movement was an urban program, and it was aimed at a kind of moral rearmament rather than at economic problems. Chiang, however, tried to refute the notion that he was neglecting the country's material needs. China's major problems were spiritual and ethical, Chiang replied to his critics.

The four virtues are the basic elements of man. If one cannot be a man, what is the use of having an abundance of food and clothing? . . . The four virtues, which rectify the misconduct of men, are the proper methods of achieving abundance. . . . People become traitors, Communists and corrupt officials, not because they are driven by hunger and cold, but because they have neglected the cultivation of virtue.

The virtues Chiang had in mind were the traditional Chinese principles usually translated as "decorum," "righteousness," "integrity," and "sense of shame." Thus the New Life Movement has generally been considered a prime example of Chiang's essential traditionalism. But this and other perversions of Chinese tradition should not be allowed to obscure the kind of conservatism Chiang and his government stood for, which was not simply traditionalism. Chiang interpreted the traditional virtues in his own way, which he insisted was a new interpretation suited to "the changing times and circumstances." An unbiased reader of the movement's literature will probably agree with Chiang that it owed more to contemporary circumstances than it did to Chinese tradition. His emphasis, for example, on the "military way of life" as a major pillar of rational living and as a manifestation of the four virtues in action probably owes more to his German advisers and his mixed respect for and fear of Japan than it does to Confucius.

The manner in which the New Life Movement was put into practice further illuminates Chiang's conception of how to adapt tradition to modern conditions; it also helps to explain why the government was unable to deal effectively with China's social needs. Lists of rules exhorted people to learn correct posture, button up their clothes, walk on the left side of the street, and take proper care of their fingernails; they were seldom taken seriously. According to one observer, "Uplifting wall slogans were posted in villages where nobody could read, and peasants who could not afford soap were lectured on the duty to wash." Exhortations that might have been taken more seriously—buy Chinese goods rather than foreign ones; kill rats, flies, and mosquitos—remained little more than exhortations. New Life Movement Promotion Associations, hundreds of which existed on paper, were inactive. Promotion of the rules was left largely to police, boy scouts, and volunteer groups. Unbelievably, a cardinal rule of operations was that the movement be carried on only in leisure hours or vacation time and not be allowed to interfere with regular duties; it relied heavily upon women's auxiliaries and students who gave up their Sunday afternoons to direct traffic or perform other services similarly designed to inculcate the four virtues. Intending to start modestly by improving individual conduct in the most ordinary everyday things and then work its way up to loftier and subtler questions of morality, the movement succeeded only in making itself a laughingstock.

After some trial and error, the movement was oriented more toward patriotic activities, public works, and health and welfare services. But it never recovered from its unfortunate beginnings, and it never reached far beyond the cities where police, students, and other volunteers could work. The movement was administered by a former YMCA secretary who was a favorite of Madame Chiang and of many Americans, but who had no talent for promoting social reform. Two years after he had initiated the movement, Chiang confessed his disappointment in its results.

To one perceptive observer, "the New Life Movement was a cherished ornament on the government's facade of Western-style progress." Before the war it cleaned up "the surface of life in the big cities" and "had results among those of the small new commercial and industrial upper class who wanted to make China like the West. In the countryside and the smaller provincial towns, however, its work was irrelevant to the point of comedy or tragedy." A scholarly analysis of the movement concludes that it was intended to imitate Japanese, German, and Italian urban practices and that it had little effect on the rural population. The New Life Movement's minimal success only widened the gap between the traditional and the modern and between the Chinese and the Western in China's agonizingly schizophrenic republican government and society.

This schizophrenia increasingly tended to be resolved in favor of the Kuomintang's brand of traditionalism. Confucian ethics competed with nationalistic Three People's Principles education even in the early days of the KMT government—Confucius' birthday became a national holiday in 1931, a Read the Classics movement was begun, and in many other ways Confucianism enjoyed a vogue in Nanking. But in 1943, with the publication of Chiang Kai-shek's *China's Destiny*, the wobbly balance between KMT traditionalism and modernism swung heavily against the modern. By this time the war was turning against Japan, and the Communists were gaining support; Chiang was more than ever preoccupied with the civil war. He set forth a reconstruction program and made an appeal to the Chinese people that dwelled at great length on foreign oppression of China and the glory of Chinese traditional culture; he denounced Western materialism and all who accepted Western ideas, especially Chinese youth, and called for a return to ancient values and old systems of group responsibility. But he also called for industrialization according to the blueprint of Sun Yat-sen. In 1943 the Western-oriented elements in China found this new KMT mixture shockingly outdated, and even businessmen found the CCP proposals more attractive than Chiang's.

ECONOMIC
DEVELOP-
MENT

Economic development requires a suitable political and social environment, but what exactly is politically and socially suitable for any particular country's economic development remains difficult to determine. Furthermore, a certain degree of economic development must precede political and social modernization in order for substantial economic development to be possible; it is sometimes argued, for example, that a considerable transportation system must exist before enough political unity can be effected in countries like China and India to enable them to industrialize. The complexity of these theoretical issues, however, need not obscure two facts about China. One fact, obvious from the preceding discussion, is that political and social conditions were decidedly unfavorable to economic development. The other is that, despite these unfavorable conditions, the economy grew and modernized considerably before 1949, but it did so in an exceedingly unbalanced manner. As a result, China in 1949 still had an essentially traditional or pre-industrial economy.

The pattern of pre-1949 economic development resembles the political and social patterns we have observed. The "modern" sector of the economy grew steadily. Railway mileage grew more than twice as rapidly between 1926 and 1937 than it had in the fifteen years before 1926, and most of the increment came between 1935 and 1937. More than 80,000 kilometers of new highways were opened (to traffic that was largely military). Industrial production in 1936, on the eve of war with Japan, was 90 percent higher than it had been in 1928 when the Kuomintang government was founded. The total number of modern banks was raised to 164 with the founding of 128 new banks between 1928 and 1937, with 1,597 branches (concentrated, of course, in the major coastal cities). In addition to such measurable gains, the government scored genuine successes in currency reform, the adoption of modern budgeting techniques, and the development of a modern banking system; and it did much to improve investment and credit mechanisms, rationalize the tax structure, and create a framework of property and contract law within which business could develop. Some of these, notably the credit and tax systems, still possessed basic weaknesses, but the government had clearly gone well beyond its predecessors in a remarkably short time.

Despite this growth, however, modern industry accounted for only about one-fiftieth of China's domestic production and did not lead to the expansion of other crucial sectors of the economy. Handicraft industry produced more than modern industry. Industry as a whole contributed only a small fraction (roughly one-tenth) of China's net domestic product; agriculture contributed about two-thirds and employed about 80 percent of the labor force. The peasants had too little land and produced too little on what they had. Because of inadequate fertilizer, seed, tools, and pest control, China's rice and wheat yields per acre were far below Japan's. Of what they did produce, tenants generally had to give about half to their landlords, and although no one knows exactly how much land was farmed by tenants, it is clear that at least half the peasants in the country suffered from one or another of the ills of tenancy —small plots, insecure tenure, high rents, usurious interest rates on loans, and the near impossibility of improving their lot. Peasants' landholdings shrank until they had barely enough to survive. According to a 1934 survey, one-third of the farms in China were smaller than 1.5 acres, and three-fourths of them were less than 5 acres. Conditions varied greatly in different parts of the country, but in the summer of 1936, according to a field study by China's leading anthropologist, the villagers' income was insufficient to secure the minimum requirements of livelihood. He concluded: "It is the hunger of the people that is the real issue in China." The KMT land law of 1930, a model piece of legislation that would have reduced rents and increased peasant landholdings, remained unenforced.

Economic development under the Kuomintang government therefore meant stagnation in agriculture, uneven but modest gains in industry, and considerable growth of modern business in some coastal areas. In general, and this is true of rural areas as well as urban, there occurred substantial *commercialization* of the economy, but very little *modernization*. In a brilliant study by G. William Skinner, it has been convincingly argued that in about 90 percent of the agrarian economy true modernization had not yet taken place by 1948. In much of the countryside, the volume of trade had increased, market towns had added additional days to their schedules, and new markets had been formed to take care of the growth in trade. But this merely expanded the old system without changing it. Only about 10 percent of the marketing areas in rural China had broken out of this pattern, become linked to major cities by modern transport facilities, and developed enough modern transportation within the area to destroy old markets.

In the cities business flourished, but industry did not. It was here that government initiative and involvement made itself felt most directly, particularly through its overwhelming control of the country's modern banks. A form of state socialism that has come to be known as "bureaucratic capitalism" permitted an inner circle of party leaders to amass private fortunes and indulge in real estate and bond speculation as well as some legitimate enterprises; other entrepreneurs found it difficult to obtain capital. Those who had capital devoted it to turning a quick profit, and little was available for the risks of investment in industry. The government's own resources went almost entirely into military spending and servicing the national debt, much of which it had inherited from its predecessors. These two items in some years took more than 80 percent of government revenues.

Finally, industry failed to develop because new industrial management and administrative techniques did not materialize. Unlike Japan's modernizers, as Franz Schurmann has aptly pointed out, Chinese entrepreneurs were unable to reconcile modern technical organization with traditional human organization. In Chinese enterprises, there was neither a separate technical organization, as in Japan, nor men who combined policy making with operational leadership.

Businessmen made decisions on money and rarely on operations. Government, officially or unofficially, provided capital but was ignorant of its use. Managers worked through gang bosses but knew little of how production was going on. Staff workers came from the educated elite; they rarely went down into the plant to observe production.

* * *

The Kuomintang could not transfer its programs and organizations from the paper they were written on to the lives of Chinese citizens. Land reform, political tutelage, local self-government, constitutionalism, and the New Life Movement remained on a display shelf that the KMT might well have labeled "Modernization by Proclamation." One hard-working and widely respected local administrator bitterly summed up his experience as of 1948: "The Nationalist government has been in power for twenty years. During these years they have said all the good words and done all the bad things. Endless talk will result in nothing."

In brief, the Kuomintang government compiled a mixed record that left China still on the threshold of modernization. By the time the KMT abandoned the mainland in 1949, modernization had proceeded extremely far in some areas of life, but in others it had barely begun. The KMT had continued the pattern of highly uneven modernization characteristic of China since the nineteenth century and had demonstrated the same inability of all Chinese governments before 1949 to develop and carry out a systematic program of modernization. In 1948 urban intellectuals still discussed the ideas of the world's great thinkers, bureaucrats drafted plans modeled on TVA, publicity men and party workers hurried through the motions of initiating a new era of constitutionalism, and businessmen watched the world market. Nearby, in areas they could see from their rooftops, little had changed. Canton was a city with a population of 1.25 million in 1948, the capital and economic center of Kuang-tung province, a major meeting point between China and the West (and with a history of foreign contact that reached back more than a millennium), a city that was in the heart of the area in which major modern revolutionary movements had erupted and from which the lion's share of Chinese overseas emigration came. Five miles from Canton, wrote a Chinese sociologist in the

1950s, "despite the increasing pace and degree of social change in the surrounding world, a process now nearly fifty years old, [the village of] Nanching up to the very eve of the victory of Chinese Communism remained essentially fixed in its traditional stable social pattern."

Chapter 4

The
Chinese Communists
on Their Way
to Power
1920–1949

When Western thought made its first deep and lasting impact on Chinese intellectuals, it impressed them with the ideas of struggle and progress. As Yen Fu had remarked, "unity and progress result from diversity and competition." Western devices for securing social cohesion seemed not to interfere with the pursuit of individual interests; national unity, wealth, and power seemed compatible with pluralism. In the early 1900s many Chinese intellectuals believed that representative government and constitutionalism ensured the best combination of unity and diversity, for Western-style democracy created strong, prosperous states and also upheld the ideals of liberty, equality, and fraternity. Hence, even though many prominent Chinese intellectuals paid attention to the Russian revolutionaries, felt some kinship with them, and became superficially acquainted with Marxism, only a few were attracted to Marxist ideas of dialectical materialism and progress by means of class struggle. The Chinese could not yet see any relationship between Marxism and national power.

Between 1912 and 1919 the intellectual and political climate changed. Because many Chinese considered that China's experiment with Western-style constitutional democracy was a dismal failure, their admiration for Western institutions wavered. The precarious balance between envy and resentment of the West tipped once again toward resentment when Westerners and Japanese violated China's territorial integrity at Versailles. Intellectuals still desperately longed for China to be both powerful and democratic, but as the failures of the republic mounted after 1912, and especially after Versailles and May Fourth, Western-style democratic politics lost much of its appeal.

During this disillusionment in China, Russia in 1917 threw off its antiquated autocracy, proclaimed scientific socialism, issued a call for world revolution, and prepared itself for both civil war and resistance to Western and Japanese efforts to crush the new Soviet regime. The Chinese watched these events as closely as they could; a few, such as the Peking University history professor and chief librarian Li Ta-chao* (1889–1927), soon commented favorably on the Bolshevik Revolution, but most were not yet touched by the events in Russia. Li began to study Marxism and to discuss it with small groups of students; among the young intellectuals who met in Li's office (which quickly became known as the "Red Chamber") was Mao Tse-tung† (1893——). Even Li, however, was still uncertain of his ideological convictions and of his estimate of the prospects for revolution. As late as spring of 1919 the mood of the intellectuals, including the most radical of them, was overwhelmingly one of curiosity, probing, and experimentation. But within a year a substantial number had turned unequivocally to Marxism-Leninism.

FOUNDING
OF THE
PARTY

Among the many reasons for this shift, three are particularly relevant to our story. The first was the renewal of political organization and activism fostered by the May Fourth Movement, with its heated anti-imperialist and antiwarlord sentiment. This two-edged nationalism, one slashing at the foreign powers and the other at the warlords who blocked the unification of China, found new meaning in Marxism-Leninism. In 1919 Lenin's writings were just beginning to become readily available to Chinese intellectuals. Works such as *Imperialism, The Highest Stage of*

---

* Pronounced *Lee Dah-jow* (as in "now").

† Pronounced *Mow* (as in "now") *Dzuh-doong*.

Capitalism, which Lenin had written only a few years before, gave the Chinese appetizing food for thought. The notions that imperialism was a necessary stage in the development of capitalism and an inherent part of capitalism and that imperialism marked the final step in capitalism's growth before it met destruction drew a deep response from the bitterly anti-imperialist intellectuals. The intellectuals' determination to find new political weapons to use against the warlords made Leninist concepts of political organization highly attractive, for the very core of Leninism was the idea of a disciplined, elite party of revolutionary intellectuals. In brief, May Fourth produced among many Chinese intellectuals sentiments that were uniquely receptive to Leninist ideas.

Another reason for the sudden growth of Marxism-Leninism in China was the Soviet Union's timely appeal to Chinese anti-imperialism. In the summer of 1919, the Soviet foreign minister declared that his government was prepared to renounce all privileges obtained from China by previous Russian governments. Later Soviet denials that the renunciation was total and revelations that the Russians were bargaining with the warlord government in Peking impressed the Chinese much less than the first and unequivocally anti-imperialist pronouncement. Praise for the Russians and salutes to the new era that had dawned in international relations filled the press. Even moderate intellectuals began to investigate Marxism, and Marxist study societies flourished as never before. Some Chinese intellectuals now sensed that Marxism-Leninism resolved one of their most agonizing dilemmas: how to be modern, Western, and scientific in their outlook and at the same time be uncompromisingly anti-imperialist, and therefore nationalist, and therefore Chinese. "Scientific socialism" in Lenin's anti-imperialist state (which was in those very years under attack by Britain, France, the United States, and Japan), offered a combination that earlier foreign objects of Chinese admiration (English liberalism, the French Revolution, United States republicanism, and Japanese modernization) could not match.

Finally, Marxism-Leninism gained impetus from the arrival of agents of the Communist International (Comintern) almost precisely when the Soviet anti-imperialist declaration was made public. With the ground already well prepared, the agents had no difficulty in persuading Ch'en Tu-hsiu to take the lead in organizing a small Communist group in Shanghai in May 1920. Other groups followed in at least five more Chinese cities, plus Tokyo and Paris. The Shanghai branch soon founded a Sino-Russian news agency, two journals, a youth corps, and a foreign language school, all aimed at recruiting and training cadres. Some cadres were later sent to the Soviet Union for advanced schooling. Only a little more than a year later the Chinese Communist Party (CCP) held its first congress, signifying the formal establishment of the party, with twelve or thirteen delegates representing an estimated fifty-seven members.

The early history of the CCP was marked by Marxist orthodoxy, adherence to a Soviet model, and subservience to outside authority. Having originated largely from the example and with the encouragement of the Soviet Union, the CCP organized itself under the watchful eyes of two Comintern representatives who attended the First Party Congress. According to one participant, the Comintern also sent a Russian worker who represented the Red International of Labor Unions and spoke to the Chinese about its aims and activities. The delegates agreed to learn from the experience and example of the Communist party of the Soviet Union. They also adopted a program that reads, appropriately enough, like a Marxist primer. To show that they meant what they said, the Communists immediately applied themselves to overthrowing "the capitalistic classes" by organizing labor unions and converting the workers into a class-conscious proletariat of which the party members might then be the vanguard. The new party set industriously to work in conventional Marxist fashion.

Perhaps the clearest indication of the CCP's lack of independence was its allegiance to the Comintern. It is likely, though not certain, that a formal affiliation between the CCP and the Comintern took place at the First Party Congress. Formally subservient or not, the CCP felt compelled to accept when the Comintern decided that the time had come to adopt a new strategy. The Comintern insisted upon an alliance with the KMT in 1923 because it believed that the CCP could in this way isolate its major enemies, the warlords and the imperialist powers; the CCP was too weak to fight alone. The Chinese Communists submitted even though they despised the KMT and were baffled by the Comintern's departure from Marxist orthodoxy. The KMT, Moscow explained, did not represent one class, the bourgeoisie; it was a coalition of all classes. Communists could therefore join it and still retain their leadership of the laboring masses. But the CCP knew it had both committed Marxist heresy and strayed from the Bolsheviks' path to power.

What sweetened this bitter pill for at least some members, including Li Ta-chao and Mao Tse-tung, was that the alliance with the KMT was aimed at ridding China of imperialism. From this point of view, subservience to the Comintern was in the larger interest of Chinese nationalism. Soon, however, Stalin relegated Chinese nationalism to a lower priority. Not merely Russian or even Comintern interests but those of Stalin himself took first place; Stalin, who was grappling with Trotsky for the right to succeed Lenin, had championed the united front policy against Trotsky's objections. Worrying less about the CCP's fate than his own, Stalin clung to the policy until Trotsky was no longer a threat to him. This, however, was a little too long for the Chinese Communists, many of whom were still clinging to it as they fell before Chiang Kai-shek's guns in 1927. Nevertheless, as Lyman P. Van Slyke has neatly put it:

It can be argued that the disaster of 1927 hid the successes that preceded it. . . . The extent of the defeat may well have been a measure of how much was attempted. . . . The CCP's rapid growth from a membership numbering a few dozen intellectuals to a mass party seriously competing for national power was an impressive accomplishment. Perhaps no set of policies could have achieved complete success in so short a time.

To build on its successes and remain a serious competitor for national power, however, the CCP found it necessary to break further with Marxist orthodoxy, Soviet models, and Comintern authority than it was able to do by 1927.

Much of Chinese Communist history centers on its transformation from a foreign-dominated movement to an essentially indigenous one. It was a twisting and erratic process in which parts of the scattered movement skidded from one pole to another like iron filings drawn this way and that by a revolving magnet. Indigenous elements were powerfully present in the beginning, and foreign influences persist to this day. But the general trend over these fifty years has been for the Chinese Communists to shape their movement to their own circumstances, take control of their own destiny, and develop their own brand of Communism.

The Chinese Communist revolution was not simply a peasant revolution; it was a revolution in which intellectuals who were disposed toward both Western and Chinese values, standards, styles of life, and conceptions of history and social relationships learned they had to bring the two together in a new way. It is not yet clear that they have done this successfully, but it is clear that they have enjoyed more success in dealing with this central problem in modern Chinese history than anyone else who has confronted it since the middle of the nineteenth century. One key to the Communists' success has been their flexibility. They have learned hard lessons and profited from them. They have formulated different types of appeals to different segments of the population and have adjusted the content and delivery of the appeal and their method of organization to changing circumstances in different parts of the country. The creativity of the Communist leadership revealed itself more in this general respect than in specific insights, such as the discovery of the revolutionary potential of the peasantry.

The importance of the peasantry had been recognized by Lenin and was perhaps seen even more clearly by Asian Communists such as the Indian M. N. Roy, who pleaded at the Second Comintern Congress in 1920 for emphasis on "mass struggle" in which peasants as well as workers would be organized by Communist parties. The Comintern itself, although often inconsistent or vague on this point, advised the CCP in May 1923 that the peasantry was "the central problem of our whole policy." In 1925 the Comintern's chief agent in China, Michael Borodin, told the KMT that organizing the peasantry for a solution of the land question would determine the success or failure of the revolution. The Comintern usually stressed, however, that the proletariat must take the lead. The question of who made the crucial intellectual breakthrough is unanswerable, but it is beyond dispute that many people realized the potential of the peasantry before anyone did much to translate that realization into political and social action, and that only after years of perseverance did the Chinese intellectuals overcome the deeply ingrained attitudes that walled them off from the Chinese masses. The difficulty of this prolonged effort, which continues even now, has profoundly influenced the Chinese Communist movement.

The work began in the 1920s, when the first serious efforts at mass mobilization were made; by turning to peasants more than to urban workers, a few pioneering Communists blazed a trail toward independence from the Comintern. The first Chinese Communist to devote himself to organizing the peasants was an intellectual who seems to have taken this course of action with little of his colleagues' hesitation. P'eng P'ai* (1896–1929) was the son of a wealthy landlord. He spent three years as a college student in Japan, where he joined a socialist group that devoted itself to agrarian problems. After graduation he returned home, joined the CCP, and soon began organizing peasants. Between May and September 1922 he organized a village peasant union with more than 500 members; four months later he organized a *hsien* Federation of Peasant Unions that claimed 20,000 members. By May 1923 he led a Kuang-tung Provincial Peasant Union which, after a temporary setback in 1924, grew to an estimated 210,000 or more, covering twenty-two *hsien*. Due partly to P'eng's success, the KMT (by now allied with the CCP) founded a Peasant Department, in which he became the most prominent individual.

---

* Pronounced *Pung Pie*.

These startling gains received little or no encouragement from the CCP, which was preoccupied with consolidating its alliance with the KMT and renewing its emphasis on organizing labor. This preoccupation was not entirely due to Marxist orthodoxy and Comintern instructions, however, for in 1924 and 1925 the labor movement expanded rapidly. There was, in other words, a good practical reason for the CCP to concentrate its efforts on urban workers—the field seemed fertile. The many strikes of 1924 and 1925 testify to the Communist organizers' success.

May Day 1925 coincidentally found both the trade unions and the peasant unions convening in Canton. The Second Labor Congress, however, dwarfed the Peasant Congress, for it represented 166 trade unions that claimed a membership of 540,000. The Peasant Congress acknowledged its subordinate role by adopting a resolution in which it affirmed that "our struggle must be concentrated in the city, because the political center is located in the city; therefore the working class must strive to lead the peasants to participate in this struggle."

By this time the CCP was beginning to take more note of the peasant movement in Kuang-tung. Party headquarters urged that peasant unions and peasant self-defense corps be organized. Such moves were invariably checked, however, because the alliance with the KMT still had top priority, and to keep that alliance the CCP had to avoid offending landlords. Hence the 1925 Peasant Congress did not dare to declare itself in favor of rent reduction. But P'eng P'ai, who did not attend the Peasant Congress, refused to accept party restraint. A few months later he urged the peasants to take matters into their own hands. They did, and many landlords and others, both innocent and guilty, lost their lives as well as their property. Reforms were at first limited to rent reduction, but soon the tenants in P'eng's area abolished rents altogether and took over the landlords' holdings. CCP membership grew from 700 in December 1926 to 4,000 only three months later, and Communist cells were created in 330 villages. Somewhat ironically, in view of the Russian desire to concentrate on the urban workers and bourgeoisie, P'eng P'ai's headquarters came to be known as "Little Moscow." More cruelly ironic was P'eng's eventual capture and execution by the KMT in Shanghai in 1929.

Earlier, however, the influence of P'eng P'ai's peasant revolution had spread north to Hu-nan. Mao Tse-tung had grown up there on a small farm that he later said had evolved to "middle peasant" range by the time he was ten years old and to "rich peasant" status later on. In 1924 Mao happened to leave his party work temporarily to return to Hu-nan; there he discovered the revolutionary potential of the peasantry and turned to rural organization work. Thanks mainly to Mao's efforts, Hu-nanese soon began to pour into P'eng P'ai's Peasant Movement Training Institute. By the autumn of 1925 Mao himself had become active in the institute, and early in 1926 he was beginning to sort out his own ideas on the relative importance of the workers and peasants. A young, inexperienced, and groping Marxist, Mao was unsuccessful in these early intellectual efforts. His writing shows a deep preoccupation with the peasants' revolutionary power, but he considered them to be only a "semi-proletariat" and held that "the industrial proletariat, though small in number, has become the major force of the national revolutionary movement."

Nevertheless Mao continued to work with the peasants, and from May to October 1926 he served as principal of the Peasant Movement Training Institute. In that capacity he once took the entire student body on a two-week visit to P'eng P'ai's headquarters to let them see first-hand a rural revolution in the making. Early in 1927 he was back in Hu-nan, where he witnessed so active a peasant movement that he predicted:

In a very short time in Central, South, and North China, several hundred million peasants will rise like a mighty storm, a hurricane, a force so swift and violent that no power, however strong, can restrain them. They will break all the shackles that bind them and rush forward along the road of liberation. All imperialists, warlords, corrupt officials, local tyrants, and bad gentry will be sent to their graves by the peasants. All revolutionary parties and comrades will stand before them to be tested and either accepted or rejected as they decide.

Mao then asked rhetorically: "Are we to march at their head and lead them? Or trail behind them, gesticulating and criticizing? Or stand in their way and oppose them?" The growth of the peasant movement in 1926 and 1927 gave Mao and a few others the answer to this question, but the Russians and the CCP leadership saw only a dilemma. To promote the peasant movement was to risk a split with the KMT; to try to check it or to find some compromise was perhaps to miss an opportunity that might not come again. The CCP managed at last to turn toward a peasant emphasis, but the shift came slowly and only at the cost of party unity. The shift was not decisive until the early 1930s, when Moscow's hand was removed and the Chinese were freer to experiment. Until that time the CCP managed to resist any temptation to exploit fully the huge reservoir of rural discontent that P'eng P'ai and Mao Tse-tung had revealed.

This important point should not be allowed to obscure the breakthrough that Chinese intellectuals in general, and the Communists in particular, made in the 1920s. Although elementary Marxist orthodoxy seemed to demand that Communists concentrate on organizing the urban proletariat, it took only a little sophistication in Marxism-Leninism to justify a policy of mobilizing the peasants; and although the Soviet experience and Comintern leadership tended to direct the Chinese to the cities, these guidelines were not fixed, and it was still possible for men like P'eng P'ai to work in the countryside and make the Comintern reconsider its strategy. The Comintern was aware of the peasants but decided its immediate interests lay more in maintaining the united front with the KMT.

The Chinese Communists had to overcome some obstacles that were inherent in Marxism-Leninism, Soviet models, and Comintern discipline, but they also had to address themselves to a central problem that all revolutionaries had to face in China: how to relate rural and urban movements to each other. In this regard their own elitism and, above all, their own inexperience and uncertainty hobbled them as much as outside control. Some, such as P'eng P'ai, found it easy to go among the peasants; most found it difficult. Mao Tse-tung himself, after having lived in cities for fifteen years, confessed that he had learned to despise rural life. Communist intellectuals found it easier to go among the workers, perhaps, but probably most of the workers were peasants only recently come from the countryside. The deeper problem was how to go among the masses, urban and rural, and mobilize them for revolution. Opportunity lay on all sides, as the huge growth of labor unions and peasant unions demonstrated. The challenge was to turn the opportunity to the service of the revolution.

In the 1920s the CCP began to meet this challenge, but the party was still too weak and inexperienced to take advantage of the opportunity, and Comintern leadership was unable to teach what the Chinese needed to know. Perhaps the mass movement was not yet large enough and the Communists' rivals, Chiang Kai-shek and the KMT, were still stronger than the CCP. Thus the CCP subordinated itself to the Comintern and gave priority to maintaining a united front with the KMT, hoping to control the KMT and, through it, to carry out a "revolution from above." But in the 1930s the CCP grew more experienced and much stronger. It freed itself of outside direction and once again rose to rival the KMT for state power, this time by mobilizing the masses in a "revolution from below."

THE RISE
OF MAO
TSE-TUNG

More than a decade after the Communists entered Peking and made it China's new capital, their foreign minister was to say: "Soviet communism has bloomed a Soviet flower and Chinese communism a Chinese one. Both are equally communism, but their flowers are of different hues." It is not clear precisely when seedlings such as those of P'eng P'ai and Mao Tse-tung blossomed fully enough to be identifiable as Chinese, but a trend toward Chinese Communist independence from Moscow is clearly identifiable in the late 1920s and thereafter becomes increasingly plain. CCP independence went hand in hand with the rise of Mao Tse-tung to leadership of the party.

Mao's rise was erratic, and his ideas as well as his strategy and tactics changed several times. Much as the nineteenth-century reformers, the earlier revolutionaries, and the Kuomintang government had shifted their ground, baffled but determined, so Mao probed and backtracked and side-

stepped and probed again. One biographer has aptly charac-
terized Mao in the late 1920s as an "apprentice Leninist."
Most students of his career would agree that his apprentice-
ship lasted rather a long time, and hostile critics find little
evidence of sophistication in his thinking to this day. But
other students of his thought see remarkable growth beginning in the 1930s. A prominent feature of that growth
was his departure from Russian models and influence.

In 1927 Chiang Kai-shek's coup left the CCP leaders
no choice but to seek their own way. Comintern policy was
thrown into confusion by Chiang's move, and by the time
it recovered the CCP was splintered into many fugitive
groups. By the beginning of 1930 there were fifteen Communist bases scattered across half of China. Each had to
survive as best it could.

Mao's struggle took him first to Hu-nan where, in
September 1927, he participated in a disastrous defeat
that may have been the most valuable learning experience
he had yet undergone. In an attempt to regain the initiative from Chiang Kai-shek, the CCP decided to attack
major cities, including Changsha in Hu-nan. Mao antici-
pated optimistically that the fall of Changsha would lead
to a successful nationwide revolution like Russia's in
1917. But until the key city fell, Mao thought, there was
no point in promoting the rural movement. A shattering
reversal at Changsha told him a new strategy was needed.

Limping into the mountains on the border of Hu-nan
and Chiang-hsi,* Mao established a base in October 1927
and began to organize it according to what he termed
his own "clumsy inventions." For about three years thereafter Mao's inventions were challenged by instructions
from the Comintern and the CCP Central Committee.
Mao objected more than once; and, although in crucial
situations he followed orders, he did so only up to a certain point. The best example is a disagreement that
matured in 1929 and 1930. By this time Mao's experience
had convinced him that the CCP's chief needs were to
establish base areas, systematically construct a political
structure, promote agrarian revolution, and build up the

---

* Pronounced *Jee-yong-hsee*.

Red Army by slow stages beginning with local militia. He also cautioned against "revolutionary impetuosity" and urged patient, but confident, preparation; he was beginning to work out the concepts of "despising one's enemy strategically, but respecting him tactically" and of surrounding cities from the countryside. The CCP leadership, however, scoffed at Mao's ideas, and the Comintern still stressed that the vital task of the CCP was to lead the struggles of urban workers. Despite this head-on collision of views, when the order came to march in a major attack on three cities, Mao and his military commander, Chu Teh* (1886———), reluctantly accepted it. But when it was evident to him that the attack was a failure, Mao did not wait for instructions to disengage. He pulled back to the Chiang-hsi base in September 1930, and from that time forward he developed and followed his own conception of how to carry the revolutionary potential of China's hinterland into her cities.

Alternatives to Mao's conception and challenges to his growing authority in the Communist movement were powerful in the years that followed. Mao was overruled on occasion, and not always to the detriment of the movement; in early 1933 Maoist tactics were abandoned, and a major victory was won by a direct frontal assault on KMT troops. Mao was criticized, and some of his adherents were vigorously attacked by the party leadership. Only in January 1935 did Mao finally gain the upper hand and make his policies those of the CCP.

Mao's policies developed in several stages, but the fundamental elements were already present by 1929 and 1930. Perhaps the innermost core of his policies was a belief in organization. A leading student of Mao, Stuart Schram, has speculated that in Mao's personality was a natural Leninism, that is, "a certain intuitive understanding of the importance of organization that is one of the reasons for his emergence as the leader of the Chinese Communist Party." Hints of this predilection appear in Mao's writings on labor organization as early as 1920 and emerge more clearly in his 1926 and 1927

---

* Pronounced *Joo Duh.*

writings on the peasantry. On several occasions in the 1920s he also demonstrated a taste and talent for analyzing organizational problems. And in Mao's own account of his efforts in 1929 to build up a base area, he recalled that the "bad tendencies" he had to correct in his followers had included "lack of discipline, exaggerated ideas of democracy, and looseness of organization." Another tendency that had to be fought was " 'vagabondage'—a disinclination to settle down to the serious tasks of government, a love of movement, change, new experience and incident." Mao had little use for spontaneity and improvisation.

Mao's remarks were directed at his troops, but he did not intend them to apply only to military organization. One of the most prominent characteristics of his outlook was the interpenetration of military and political strategy. In 1929, for example, Mao explicitly condemned what he termed "the purely military viewpoint." He explained:

[The Red Army] is an armed group for carrying out political tasks of a class nature. In order to carry out this task, particularly in present-day China, the Red Army must not merely fight; besides fighting, it should also shoulder such important tasks as agitating among the masses, organizing them, arming them, and helping them to set up political power. When the Red Army fights, it fights not merely for the sake of fighting but exclusively to agitate among the masses, to organize them, to arm them, and to help them establish political power; apart from such objectives, fighting loses its meaning, and the Red Army the reason for its existence.

Mao then went on to explain why "absolute equalitarianism" in the army was essentially the same as "extreme democratization in political matters" and equally reprehensible. In brief, similar principles governed military and political matters, and the purpose of military organizing was to create political organization. The classic and by now the most familiar expression of these concepts is Mao's statement in 1938 that "political power grows out of the barrel of a gun." The statement continues: "Our principle is that the Party commands the gun: the gun shall never be allowed to command the Party. . . . Anything can grow out of the barrel of a gun. . . . As advocates of the abolition of war, we do not desire war; but war can only be abolished through war—in order to get rid of the gun we must first grasp it in hand."

Since Mao was engaged in war almost continually from 1927 to 1953, this experience inevitably molded his thinking and infiltrated his idiom. Mao's stress on military power and his use of military terminology is in no way surprising. More remarkable is the persistent reference to the political context of military affairs. Even during the life-or-death struggle against Japan, Mao said: "Any tendency among the anti-Japanese soldiers to belittle politics, to isolate war from it, and to make war an absolute, is erroneous and must be corrected." Although Mao conceded that "war has its special characteristics and in this sense it is not identical with politics," he insisted,

such a gigantic national revolutionary war as ours cannot succeed without universal and thoroughly political mobilization. . . . The popular masses are like water, and the army is like a fish. How then can it be said that when there is water, a fish will have difficulty in preserving its existence? An army which fails to maintain good discipline gets into opposition with the popular masses, and thus by its own actions dries up the water. In this case, it naturally cannot continue to exist. All guerrilla units must thoroughly understand this principle.

Thus Mao closed the circle around his core ideas. Base areas were the water in which he would find his fish and from which he would feed them. A revolutionary land program would attract peasant support, and disciplined troops would preserve it. Soldiers recruited from the peasantry would feel they had a stake in protecting the base areas; indeed, a local defense corps would provide a way of initiating peasants into organized activity and solidifying their sense of common purpose. Mao insisted that *all* people had to be included, even bandits and other unreliable elements, of whom there were many in Mao's original force. Not only were they to be included, they were to be given education and made to feel deeply involved. It was not enough for people to learn of the war by being subjected to enemy action. The people needed the positive message of the Red Army, not merely the negative one of the Japanese. Finally, "with the common people of the whole country mobilized, we shall create a vast sea of humanity in which the enemy will be swallowed up, [we shall] obtain relief for our shortage in arms and other things, and secure the prerequisites to overcome every difficulty in the war."

The actual course of the Chinese Communists' rise to power followed Mao's policies with considerable precision, although deviations were inevitable under the harsh and changing conditions of those years. In Chiang-hsi in the early 1930s there were also disagreements within the party that interfered with consistency, especially at this early stage in the process of building a base area. But by 1935 the rise of Mao and the rise of Chinese communism had become irrevocably meshed.

YENAN
COMMUNISM

After the Chinese Communists were forced by Kuomintang military pressure to flee the Chiang-hsi area, they took refuge in the northwest. The relocation required what came to be known as the "Long March," an epic trek of a full year over some 6,000 miles of fiercely hostile terrain. Along the way the Communists fought at great loss against pursuing government armies and local warlord forces, but Mao claimed that they had also "sown many seeds in eleven provinces, which will sprout, grow leaves, blossom into flowers, bear fruit and yield a crop in future."

The Long March began the next stage of CCP history, commonly called the "Yenan* period." Yenan did not become the CCP's northwest capital until January 1937, but the Yenan period is usually delimited by the end of the Long March in 1935 and the end of the civil war in 1949. During that time Mao consolidated his power within the party and promoted new ideological emphases on the power of the human will to do the seemingly impossible and on the distinctiveness of the Chinese revolution. These

---

* Pronounced *Yeh-non,* the first syllable resembling "yet" without a "t."

emphases characterize the "Yenan spirit," to which the Long March is a fitting prologue. The march was an extraordinary test of endurance, will power, determination, and self-reliance. It brought the CCP into direct contact with parts of the country that few party members had ever seen and ended by putting the CCP in a position to fight against the invading Japanese, on whom they had declared war in April 1932. Thus the march stimulated patriotic feeling by providing the Communists with a broader knowledge of their country and an opportunity to fight for it. It is entirely possible that the Yenan spirit was born as a result of the Long March.

The first clear indication of new emphases in Mao's thinking came very shortly after the Long March. In 1936 Mao wrote an essay on China's strategic problems in which he minimized the value of Russian experience as an example for the CCP.

Although we must value Soviet experience, and even value it somewhat more than experiences in other countries throughout history, because it is the most recent experience of revolutionary war, we must value even more the experience of China's revolutionary war, because there are a great number of conditions special to the Chinese revolution and the Chinese Red Army.

These special conditions determined that the Chinese revolution would be distinctive. First, China was a semicolonial country, controlled by several imperialist powers; Mao refrained from pointing out that Russia, far from being colonized, had been imperialist herself. Second, China was unevenly developed politically and economically. It had only small classes of industrial workers and capitalists but vast numbers of peasants, only a few semimodern industrial and commercial cities but "boundless expanses of rural districts still stuck in the middle ages." Warlords and warlord armies divided the country, but the KMT was strong and gaining in strength. Above all, the KMT held "the key positions or lifelines in the politics, economy, communications and culture of China." These conditions compelled the CCP to lead China in a revolutionary war different from the relatively brief civil war in the Soviet

Union after the 1917 revolution. China had to plan for a protracted war. Furthermore, the Chinese Red Army had to face two enemies, Japan and the KMT, both of whom had armies that were far larger and more modern than the Communists' force. The Red Army could win, Mao said, "because its men have sprung from the agrarian revolution and are fighting for their own interests, and because officers and men are politically united." According to Mao's estimates the CCP could win by relying on itself; it needed neither foreign aid nor models. But he stressed that the war would be long and difficult and might even be lost.

From 1936 on, Mao concentrated on developing a winning strategy. The problem of fighting the Japanese and simultaneously preparing to fight the KMT absorbed him completely. He reasoned that to fight well, the Red Army had to be a people's army, and to be a people's army it needed a program uniquely suited to Chinese conditions.

The conditions Mao outlined were not entirely unique to China; Russia's Red Army, for example, had also faced both foreign and domestic troops that possessed superior numbers and equipment. But China's economy was far less developed than Russia's had been in 1917, and China had a far smaller urban working class; still more important, the Chinese Communists had failed to gain a foothold in the cities, whereas the Bolsheviks' power was rooted in Moscow, Petrograd, and a few other industrial cities. Finally, and perhaps most important of all, the Bolsheviks gained followers by calling for peace in World War I and surrendering to Germany huge pieces of Russian territory; the Chinese Communists gained followers by calling for resistance to Japan and leading the fight to defend Chinese territory.

Thus one of the most important differences between China and the Soviet Union emerged only after Mao made his analysis. The Chinese Red Army grew from roughly 80,000 to about a million during the war against Japan, and in addition to these regular troops the CCP by 1945 commanded guerrilla forces and militia that amounted to several million more. These huge forces were unlike any soldiers the Chinese masses could remember. The people were accustomed to soldiers who looted and raped. The Red Army became famous for its honesty and discipline. Relying exclusively on volunteers, it became a people's army in the fullest sense of that term. And because its training was at least as much political as military, the Red Army was a school in which countless peasants learned to read, think about national goals, and work for the victory of communism as well as of China.

In 1938 Mao wrote:

A communist is a Marxist internationalist, but Marxism must take on a national form before it can be applied. . . . We must put an end to writing eight-legged essays [old-fashioned essays that have perfect form but no substance] on foreign models; there must be less repeating of empty and abstract refrains; we must discard our dogmatism and replace it by a new and vital Chinese style and manner, pleasing to the eye and to the ear of the Chinese common people.

To reach the eye and ear of the common people in a Chinese manner, the CCP during the Yenan period adopted a variety of policies that shifted according to time and place; Mao and his followers continued to demonstrate a flexibility that was vital to their success. The policies were based on patriotic resistance to Japan, a program of land reform that concentrated on reducing rents and interest rates, and a system of local government that resembled, at least in form, parliamentary democracy. These policies of moderation helped the CCP to earn a reputation as nationalists and democratic "agrarian reformers."

To carry out these diverse policies, Mao relied heavily upon a single technique, the "mass line." The idea underlying this technique has been summed up most simply by Chalmers Johnson: In order to find out what kind of political program the masses will support, a political leader goes among them and asks them. The concept of the mass line is itself fundamentally simple, but the CCP's efforts to implement it reveal an enormous complexity. The mass-line policy requires CCP members to reconcile what the masses *will* support with what the party in its Marxist-Leninist wisdom thinks they *should* support; once these two rarely matching designs have been stitched together, party members must take the finished products back to the people and, in the words of one leader, "explain and popularize them, and arouse the masses to support these policies *so they will act on them as their own.*" Italics have been added to indicate it was in this respect that the CCP did the most to refashion in its own way what is in reality a rather common notion; and, by so doing, the CCP grew by leaps and bounds during the Yenan period. Through its highly imaginative formulation and skilled execution of a mass-line technique adapted to Chinese conditions, the CCP came to power.

Following the mass-line technique, the CCP sent agents into countless villages. There the agents listened, learned the peasants' grievances, gained their confidence, and tried to explain why the grievances existed and what could be done to erase them. With the party's active encouragement, peasants found the courage to pursue their own interests whether those interests were to regain land they had lost due to usury or high rents, take revenge on a corrupt official, or resist the Japanese occupation. As they corrected old abuses and mobilized to defend their homes, the peasants accepted CCP leadership and organization. Some began to absorb communist ideas, for the CCP taught many people to read and did so with heavy doses of propaganda that began in the early lessons. Creating new organs of local government, peasant associations, cooperatives, youth and women's organizations, and militia, the Chinese Communists drew unprecedented numbers of the Chinese people into purposeful action.

The CCP was not the only group to perceive patriotism, anti-imperialism, land reform, mass education, and political democracy as desirable ends. Throughout the twentieth century one movement after another had proclaimed these and other laudable goals. But no other group so carefully defined goals with an eye to what the masses of people wanted, and no other group so assiduously cultivated the ability to mobilize the masses in pursuit of those ends. Here is where the Communists are most clearly distinguished from all other political groups in modern Chinese history, for it was the CCP in the Yenan period that at last, even if only temporarily, bridged the gap between city and country, modern and traditional, Western and Chinese, rulers and ruled. As a result, China made a fresh start in her struggle to modernize.

During the eight years of war against Japan and, concurrently, intermittent fighting against the KMT, the CCP's strategy and methods were put to a severe test. Genuine unity still required that Western-oriented modern urban intellectuals come directly to grips with the problems of rural and still largely traditional China. New personnel problems appeared as Communist influence expanded to reach more than 100 million people in 1945, at least one hundred times more people than it reached in 1936. The Communist areas virtually amounted to a huge, sprawling nation (the population of the United States in 1945 was about 140 million). Numerous Communist enclaves were scattered over vast areas, and it was nearly impossible to maintain contact between them and Yenan; local party workers had to be reliable because they often had to work without instructions. The Communists needed more manpower to carry out the mass line; hence party membership grew from 40,000 in 1937 to over 1,200,000 in 1945. According to CCP historians, 90 percent of the new members were from "petty bourgeois" backgrounds. Precisely when the party needed experienced and reliable cadres, it also had to grow rapidly, and it had no choice but to admit untested members and try to train them quickly; both quality and quantity were urgently necessary. A party leader warned that "nonproletarian classes" were influencing the CCP in "ideology, living habits, theory, and action." By 1940 CCP membership had shot up to about 800,000; party organization and mobilization of the masses were in danger of being crippled by excessively rapid expansion. Setbacks in 1941 and 1942, due to Japanese offensives and a Kuomintang blockade, heightened the sense of urgency and the need for cadres who were dedicated enough to start their work again after a defeat. The leadership followed two courses. One was to slow down party recruitment, weed out the less desirable members, and indoctrinate intensively those who remained. The other was to simplify administration, develop local leadership, and introduce new social and economic institutions, such as cooperatives, on an unprecedentedly wide scale. The first worked from the top (government) down; the second worked from the bottom (villages) up.

Indoctrination was undertaken on a massive scale from 1942 to 1944, based on a small body of written materials, mostly Mao's, which were widely disseminated, studied, and discussed. The central theme was a reaffirmation and strengthening of Mao's 1936 statement that the Chinese revolution posed its own unique and concrete problems and that men had to engage those problems in hand-to-hand combat. The bedrock of the entire new movement was Mao's demand, stated in a lecture he gave in 1942, for "a theory in accordance with China's real necessities, a theory which is our own and of a specific nature." Another leader, Liu Shao-ch'i* (1900———), explained further the Chinese effort to "make something real of Marxism." The CCP, he said,

has passed through many more great events in these twenty-two years [since 1921] than any other Communist Party in the world and has had richer experience in the Chinese revolutionary struggle. If we treat the experience of our Party's struggle in these twenty-two years of great historical change lightly, if we do not diligently learn our lessons from these experiences, but only learn the lessons of the revolutionary experience of comparatively distant foreign countries, we will be turning things upside down and will have to travel many tortuous paths and encounter many more defeats.

Artfully invoking the authority of Stalin, Liu quoted a lengthy statement in which the Russian leader's point was that "true Marxists" are only those who are "guided by methods and procedure in keeping with their environment" and who "do not find their instructions and directives from comparisons and historical analogies," but from "research on surrounding conditions" and from their own "practical experience."

The stress on "practical experience" served to underline the uniquely Chinese emphases of the CCP leaders, and it also honed the blade Mao used to lacerate the intellectuals:

---

* Pronounced *Lee-oo Show* (rhymes with "now") -*chee*.

"I advise those of you who have only book knowledge and as yet no contact with reality, and those who have had few practical experiences, to realize your own shortcomings and make your attitudes a bit more humble." Humility was taught not only with Mao's advice, but also by means of a "to the village" movement that followed the indoctrination. After mastering the selected texts, intellectuals were sent to the countryside, sometimes to work in the fields, sometimes to teach and to aid in local administration. At all times, Mao warned, such "outside cadres" must take care to "cherish, protect, and constantly assist local cadres" and "not ridicule or attack them"; and all cadres "must actually learn from the people."

An excellent example of the CCP's emphasis on practicality and mass initiative can be seen in its educational system. At first, schools in the Communist areas followed familiar Western practices. In the border area of Shen-hsi, Kansu, and Ningsia-hui, however, the masses protested that education did not suit their needs. The CCP investigated in order to determine what kind of schools people wanted, and the result was the establishment of "people-managed" schools in which each village decided what should be taught. Problems of many kinds were inevitable—some villages even wanted to stress the Confucian classics, and in such cases the authorities had to persuade the village committee that classical learning was impractical—but the system proved to be so popular that in 1944 it spread quickly throughout the Communist areas. Literacy, arithmetic, and vocational subjects predominated, the general rule being that mass education "should keep to the knowledge needed by the home and the village." Cadre education, which stressed leadership in both warfare and production, was conducted by "people who actually have experience of the armed struggle or production."

This educational system also exemplified the CCP's determination to dispense with foreign models that did not suit Chinese conditions. Party directives criticized the KMT for copying Western and Japanese education, referring frequently to the differences between China and countries that were wealthy, industrialized, capitalist, and at peace. One crucial difference, for example, was China's extensive adult illiteracy, which impaired her ability to increase production rapidly and at the same time carry on a protracted people's war. Since adults had greater responsibilities than youth, the CCP decided to give adults priority over children in the mass education campaign.

*   *   *

The success with which these principles were carried out in the Yenan period is indicated by the dramatic reversal of the Communist-Kuomintang balance. A bedraggled remnant in 1935, the CCP scratched at the barren soil of the northwest and looked out from its caves upon a future as bleak as the land; meanwhile, the resurgent KMT seemed capable of destroying its enemy with only another blow. Ten years later the CCP not only was in a position to challenge the KMT for power and win, but it had tangible skills and intangible momentum and spirit to carry it into the postrevolutionary era.

The spirit may have developed most of all from the war effort, which was the immediate objective of all other policies. Many of the policies, including mass propaganda and village organization, were implemented through the army, especially in the early years of the war. As trained party workers were produced, they took up more of the burden. But whoever was responsible for the implementation of policy, the spirit was essentially the same. Peasants who had been intimidated by the air power and tanks of Japan's war machine learned to their astonishment that it was possible to fight back by guerrilla methods; at the same time, many learned to read, to command troops, to govern, and to produce more than ever from their land. Mao taught that nothing was impossible for men who combined practical experience, understanding of Marxism-Leninism and the thought of Mao Tse-tung, and the will to undertake awesome tasks in a spirit of optimism: "So when we see the enemy, whether he is many or few, we must act as though he is bread which can satisfy our hunger, and immediately swallow him." This kind of confidence flourished in the climate of patriotic resistance to invasion. Peasants and intellectuals knew what they were fighting for and became certain they would win. Differences of social class, wealth, and education were outweighed by a new unity of purpose. By 1945 this spirit motivated countless cadre teams like the one in Stone Wall Village; it also welded the dispersed Red areas into a nation within a nation.

In the civil war that followed from 1946 to 1949, the Chinese Communists won a victory that was even more their own than the victory over Japan. Two stunning military successes against huge mechanized armies vindicated the strategy of people's war. But, as in Stone Wall Village, the strategy had also unleashed a social revolution. Would the Communists carry it forward in the pattern of the preceding decade? If so, Mao's strategy would undergo its severest test yet, for it would have to adapt the techniques of people's war to the tasks of government.

Chapter 5

The
Chinese Communists
in Power
1949-1971

Successful revolutionaries face their greatest challenges only when they have succeeded in taking power. The transition from "outsiders" seeking power to "insiders" exercising power is a giant, slippery step into unknown territory. The Chinese Communists were in many ways better equipped than other revolutionaries, including the Russians, to manage this transition. Unlike the Russians when they came to power, the Chinese Communists had had considerable experience in governing large, heavily populated areas and a long history of continuing and coherent leadership. Because of this experience and their belief in the importance of being guided by their own experience, a continuity was to be expected between their policies and methods before and after 1949. In 1945 Mao Tse-tung said that the Chinese Communists would not follow the Soviet Union's example after they came to power. "Russian history has created the Russian system," he said, but "Chinese history will create the Chinese system." In 1949, however, new circumstances compelled Mao to declare, "the Communist Party of the USSR is our best teacher from whom we must learn."

The new circumstances Mao observed in 1949 were created by the Chinese Communists' rapid conquest of the entire country. Between November 1948 and January 1949 the last decisive battles of the civil war were fought. All of China was soon in Communist hands. In April 1949 the Red Army, which three years earlier had been renamed the People's Liberation Army (PLA), crossed the Yangtze River; within another month the PLA swept into major cities of northern and central China, including Sian, Wuhan, and Shanghai; and between October and December 1949 the army captured Canton in the southeast and Chengtu in the southwest. In the short space of about two and one-half years of civil war, the CCP took responsibility for governing 500 million more people than it had governed in 1946.

As his troops consolidated their hold on north China and began to fan out to the south in February 1949, Mao told them:

The formula followed in the past twenty years, "first the rural areas, then the cities," will be reversed and changed to the formula, "first the cities, then the rural areas." . . . In short, you should from now on shoulder all urban problems, with which our army cadres and fighters were unfamiliar in the past. . . . Since in the south all the rural areas will be newly liberated, the work will be fundamentally different from that in the old liberated areas of the north. . . . Therefore, rural work must also be learned afresh. However, as compared with urban work, rural work is easy to learn. Urban work is more difficult and is the main subject you are studying. If our cadres cannot quickly master the administration of cities, we shall encounter extreme difficulties.

Mao realized that the CCP's past experience, though valuable, was an insufficient guide for the new government. The CCP's experience prior to 1949 had been dominated by large-scale warfare and the administration of a dispersed rural population. The CCP had never governed large urban populations or dealt extensively with rural-urban relations and had never confronted economic problems on the gigantic scale of those awaiting it in 1949. It is not surprising that in 1949 Mao chose once again to look to the Soviet Union's thirty years of experience as an organized government for a model; rather it is testimony to his ability to assess situations in a rationally calculated manner even when the assessment forced him to unpalatable conclusions.

The conclusions Mao drew in 1949 were unpalatable because the Soviet model gave high priority to nationwide economic planning, relied heavily upon centralized administration, and stressed the use of advanced technology. Probably none of these policies were wholly repugnant to Mao, but some of their implications were distasteful to him. For example, his guerrilla experience had given him a deep distrust of centralization. Guerrilla units in scattered base areas had to rely very much on themselves because communications were too poor and conditions too changeable to permit very much coordination from Yenan. In 1949 Mao must not have been optimistic about the possibility of bringing the entire country under a highly centralized direction. This conclusion was probably reinforced by his knowledge that the problem of balancing central control and local autonomy figured so prominently in Chinese history. China resembles a continent, and her twenty-nine major administrative units are like countries—each of eight provinces has more people than Poland, and each of twelve others has more people than East Germany. Most of these areas had only now come under CCP control, and in many of them lived minority nationalities whose customs and languages were unfamiliar to the Communists. South China was also divided by countless mutually unintelligible local dialects. Unity was only a thin membrane covering the countryside, which was still fixed in a traditional decentralized social and political pattern. That "scattered sand" to which Sun Yat-sen had likened the Chinese people remained to be cemented into a nation.

The reservations Mao had about the Soviet model were outweighed by clear advantages. The Russians were at least ideological cousins and offered aid. In December, 1949, Mao went to Moscow. After two months of bargaining, the Soviet Union agreed to provide loans and technical advisers. It made sense for Russian advisers to teach what they knew best, and they may have demanded Chinese conformity as their price. China's people, weary of war and economic chaos, yearned for peace and stability; since nearly a century of deep political division had to be overcome, some centralization seemed unavoidable, despite its dangers. Unity was essential if China was to maintain her security and independence, mobilize her resources for industrialization, and advance to socialism and communism.

Mao had to find a new balance that would put more weight on central direction than on local authority, and greater centralization would force him to deal with another age-old problem, bureaucratization. Mao knew that this affliction, too, had plagued imperial China, and he had seen with his own eyes how it had crippled Chiang Kai-shek's government. Communist doctrine and Soviet experience also warned him that state machinery inevitably became bureaucratic and alienated from the masses. A firm believer that "reality" did not exist in books or in paperwork, but out in the fields and battlegrounds where the crucial work had to be done, Mao was not likely to drop his guard against bureaucratism.

Centralization posed other challenges to Mao's beliefs. The more stress he placed on central direction, the more he would have to rely not merely on bureaucrats, but on experts of all kinds. If China was to industrialize, there would be a special need for scientists, engineers, technicians, and other such educated people. The need for an intellectual elite went strongly against Mao's populist, anti-elitist, anti-intellectual beliefs; it also went against the mystique, built up in Yenan days, that the mobilization of the masses was the solution to the seemingly insoluble. Mao's distaste for relying heavily on an intellectual elite was reinforced by the knowledge that China's intelligentsia came mostly from bourgeois backgrounds; to him this meant they were contaminated by the acquisitiveness and other bourgeois values of the so-called liberal-democratic West that he detested. He recognized that he needed the intellectuals, but he vowed to change them. Here too the Soviet experience would be helpful to the Chinese.

Thus the new government set out upon the road to socialism in 1949, consciously (but not without reservations) following guideposts planted by the Soviet Union. The CCP had turned a sharp corner; however, it had by no means reversed itself. Although the Chinese had taken power by means of their own resources and, unlike the Russians, had done so by waging a protracted war in the countryside that only after many years enveloped the urban areas, much Russian influence had survived in the CCP. The Chinese had gone far toward developing their own unique ideology, party structure, party-army relations, and mass organizations, but the Soviet heritage was still present. In 1949, in other words, the Chinese Communist movement was not fully Sinified. Furthermore, the decision in 1949 to follow Soviet models did not at all preclude continuing modification of alien borrowings, nor did it preclude a return to deliberate Sinification.

TOWARD
SOCIALIST
CONSTRUC-
TION

The Chinese did not move immediately to introduce socialism. In an essay titled "On New Democracy," Mao in 1940 had explained that the Chinese revolution was occurring in two stages: democracy and socialism. These stages were to be reached by means of two different revolutionary processes, he said, and the second could not begin until the first had been completed. In 1949 China was not yet ready to move into socialism. The stage of "New Democracy," which Mao had carefully defined as "democracy of the Chinese type, a new and special type," therefore remained to be fulfilled, and Mao had specified that it would exist for "quite a long time." Under New Democracy, large business and industrial enterprises would be owned and managed by the state, but there would be no general confiscation of private property, and not all capitalist production would be discouraged. In the countryside a "rich peasant economy" would be allowed, and only some cooperatives containing "elements of socialism" would be developed. These principles Mao mostly reaffirmed in 1949: "Our present policy is to regulate capitalism, not to destroy it." One important difference from 1940 was that then Mao had called for a joint dictatorship of all revolutionary classes; in 1949, perhaps because of his new orientation toward the cities, Mao stressed the leadership of the industrial working class: "it is only the working class that is most far-sighted, most selfless, and most thoroughly revolutionary."

For about three years after 1949 the Chinese Communist

Party stressed consolidation and rehabilitation of China. Conciliatory policies were particularly evident in 1949 and 1950 in the cities, which the CCP thought were so foreign that they had to be "truly Sinified." Runaway inflation was checked, the economy revived on a mixed basis in which the "capitalist" (or private ownership) component was surprisingly prominent, and a new political system gathered in the loose reins of administration. Working primarily through city police forces, which became the first instrument of urban civil administration, the CCP gradually restored order. It then began to organize urban dwellers in their places of employment and residence to publicize its policies, carry out the various tasks of government such as sanitation and fire prevention, and mobilize support for party policies.

Basic to all these measures was a massive campaign to recruit party members and cadres, especially among the urban working class but also among intellectuals and other "bourgeois elements." In 1949 the membership of the CCP was about 4.4 million, of which about 80 percent were peasants, 5 percent intellectuals, and almost none industrial workers. By 1956, when the party had nearly tripled in size, the percentages were 67, 12, and 14, respectively; since 86 percent of China's population was rural, the peasantry had become underrepresented in the party between 1949 and 1956, while urban workers and intellectuals had made relatively greater gains.

Mao wished not to imprison urban intellectuals and businessmen but to employ their talents to build a new regime. Few were treated harshly at the very outset; most were offered a chance to make their peace with the CCP. For many, this chance turned out to be a painful experience in which they were subjected to "ideological remolding" or "thought reform" (sometimes misleadingly called "brainwashing"), economic penalties, public scorn and mistreatment, and sometimes eventually imprisonment, exile, or death. Nevertheless, many people who had reason to fear merciless treatment by the government managed instead to find places for themselves in it. Thought reform played an important role in this accommodation process.

Thought reform consists essentially of two parts. The

first part is a person's admission that he or she has done wrong in the past and now renounces all such errors; the second is the acquisition of "correct" thinking. Chinese methods of conducting thought reform have evolved over a long period of time and are still changing; for this reason, and because many myths and exaggerated fears have grown up concerning brainwashing, brief descriptions of it are inadequate. For our purposes it needs to be stressed that the theory and practice of thought reform represent a highly complex mixture of Soviet experience, the Chinese Communists' own experience (especially in the Yenan period), and some ancient Chinese traditions (although it has also been aimed at destroying some traditional ideas). Two differences between Russian and Chinese practices are striking. One difference is that the Chinese came to regard thought reform as a more important means of effecting intellectual change than the conventional Marxist-Leninist means. Traditionally, Marxists have believed that fundamental intellectual change comes about primarily as a result of economic change; only when a socialist economy is established will people's minds be truly purged of capitalist or bourgeois ideas. Mao, however, came to believe that thought reform can be effective independent of socialism, and signs of this belief are discernible in his early efforts to remold the ideology of Chinese intellectuals. A second difference is one of relative emphasis: the Chinese have relied much more than the Russians did on thought reform and persuasion and less than they on naked force to effect social and cultural change.

Although thought reform was an uncompromising assault upon old ideas and values, designed to wash away "contaminated" beliefs, some Chinese intellectuals found relief from old doubts and tensions in the new principles it taught. Most important, thought reform gave those who were able to profit from it a new sense of group identity and common purpose and a feeling of participating in a crusade to reform society. Even some who rebelled against thought reform later felt guilty for abandoning the crusade.

For a year or two, Chinese cities enjoyed what one scholar has termed an "atmosphere of permissiveness."

Moderate and stabilizing policies began to change as early as the autumn of 1950, when China entered the Korean War. Before the end of the year, a "Resist-America–Aid-Korea" campaign was sweeping the Chinese mainland. Designed to mobilize popular support for the war, the campaign began as an intense patriotic movement to recruit volunteers for the army. Gradually it broadened into campaigns to raise money, increase production, suppress counterrevolutionaries, revolutionize the land system, reform the government and party, and wrest control of the urban economy from businessmen. Fears of possible attack by the United States or sabotage and subversion from within played some part, but the campaigns soon went far beyond security needs. The authorities felt that, because business was flourishing, people who worked in urban enterprises, including many CCP members, had become too complacent and self-seeking. Late in 1951, therefore, the CCP began a series of massive purges known as the "Three-anti" and "Five-anti" movements. Among the major targets were cadres, government officials, managers of state-operated enterprises, and those private businessmen and industrialists who were still operating.

These campaigns led to an increasing socialization of industry and commerce; state control of the economy, in turn, permitted the centralized planning needed for a Soviet-style Five-Year Plan. China's first such plan was initiated in 1953. Stressing industry far more than agriculture, heavy industry far more than light, and large enterprises far more than small, the plan faithfully followed the goals and methods of the Soviet Union. Industrial production grew remarkably from 1953 to 1957, and with the success of the first Five-Year Plan, China seemed to have left behind the era of New Democracy that Mao had proclaimed in 1940; in industry, at least, the era of socialist construction had begun.

In the countryside there was a less uniform pattern and a somewhat less faithful adherence to the Soviet example, but there too socialization began to prevail by 1953. The Communists had carried out land reform in some areas of China before they occupied the entire country. After 1949 land reform became a part of the CCP's program of consolidation and rehabilitation; it was a means of making good on old promises, restoring order in the countryside, and establishing a foundation for nursing the shattered economy back to health.

The CCP's first task was to plant itself in every one of China's villages, but China had only one civilian cadre for every two villages. It was clearly impossible to duplicate the Yenan pattern of sending cadres to penetrate the villages, and for a few years party influence in the rural areas was accordingly quite limited. In most places formal administration reached down only to the township, one level below the *hsien*. The government was not yet able to live up to its stated commitment "to forge closer ties between the government and the masses."

The party's efforts in this direction persisted. From 1950 to 1955, as more cadres graduated from the training institutes, the larger townships were steadily broken up into smaller ones. The general principle was to bring the size of the township, and therefore its government, as close to the village level as the availability of trained, reliable cadres allowed. By 1955 there were a little over 200,000 townships in China, roughly five times the number that had existed in 1949. The average size of the basic unit of administration was about three thousand people.

During the same period, while the political administrative network was stretching down from the *hsien* and townships to the masses, another network was beginning to grow up from the villages. Mass organizations of peasants, youth, and women had been created in each village following the entrance of the People's Liberation Army. Usually under the direction of military cadres, these mass organizations were intended to promote popular participation in local affairs, particularly in land reform. As the military cadres were gradually replaced by civil authority, the CCP's shortage of trained personnel compelled it to rely on "outsiders" (non-village or urban people) to oversee land reform. One observer gave this report on the cadres sent to a village near Canton:

The land reform cadres in Nanching, three men and one woman in their late teens or early twenties, were high school graduates, and one seemed from the way he talked to have had one or two years of college. Their manners and conversation revealed an urban bourgeois background which they carefully disguised under dirty gray uniforms and conscious attempts to imitate the peasants' mode of life, occasionally even living in the poor peasants' houses, eating their food, and helping with light farm chores in order to strike up a conversation with them for information about the village.

The eager but inexperienced young cadres made their share of mistakes, such as choosing "middle peasants" instead of poor farmers or agricultural laborers to head the peasant associations responsible for land reform, but land reform was completed nevertheless. Large holdings were broken up, and about 125 million acres of land were redistributed among small owners, former tenants, and farm laborers. Private ownership and "rich peasants" flourished for a time. By the end of 1952 the CCP had completed land reform in most areas.

During the course of completion the party sent in thousands of outside cadres to reinforce its local personnel and weed out recalcitrants. The cadres learned who the activists and potential leaders of the villages were and made a special effort to draw them into party service. New local leadership was thereby created, and the peasant associations became firmly established as centers of village power. The associations excluded rich peasants and former landlords and were headed by local activists chosen by the cadres. Thus the CCP overturned the old village power structure and, through local activists, established its authority in the village.

For the most part, the CCP resorted to violence only in areas where the Kuomintang forces or sympathizers contested the Communist takeover and defended the established order. Estimates of how many landlords died vary widely, but there was less violence than many expected, given the enormity of the land problem; the problem was especially great in southern China, where tenancy was far more widespread than in the north. Whatever the precise level of violence in each area, land reform constituted a vast social revolution that reduced the old rural elite to near impotence.

By 1952, in addition to the economic and social purposes it served, land reform had also helped to solve a major political problem—the reassertion of central control over outlying regions. By promoting land reform, the CCP was able to extend its control throughout the countryside; and, as Ezra Vogel has found for Kuang-tung province, land reform "transformed a semi-autonomous guerrilla organization into a disciplined local outpost of a strong central administration." Land reform thus laid the foundations both for collectivization and for a unified administrative system.

The first stage of collectivization began soon after peasant associations were formed. Whenever *hsien* authorities deemed that enough local leaders were available, the peasants were sufficiently receptive, and other conditions were suitable, they ordered the establishment of mutual aid teams. These were small groups averaging about five families who retained their individual land and possessions but who exchanged labor and shared tools and animals. By 1952 about 40 percent of the peasants were members of mutual aid teams. In February 1953 the CCP ordered this simple and rather informal cooperation expanded into farms called Agricultural Producers Cooperatives (APC). These averaged about twenty-five families, but there were some with as many as fifty, seventy, or one hundred families. In the APCs, family holdings were pooled, boundary markers destroyed, and the entire holding of all families cultivated as a single farm.

At first the CCP applied only moderate pressure to form cooperatives, and after two years only 13.5 percent of the peasants were in them. To encourage the growth of cooperatives, township officials and local cadres went out to the countryside to explain the advantages and to organize them. By offering the peasants substantial material inducements, the officials and cadres had some success in promoting APCs, and in the process they strengthened their own relationship with the peasants. With each APC that was organized, the township administration established itself a little more firmly among the peasants. The forging of such links between officialdom and masses was not smooth. Twice the drives to promote APCs had to be called off; in one area one-third of the nine thousand APCs had to be either dissolved or reduced to mutual aid teams. A central problem was the poor quality of the local cadre leadership; the most common complaint was that excessive use of coercion had alienated the peasants. Many local cadres came from landlord, "rich peasant," or bourgeois backgrounds, or they had friends and relatives who did. Therefore, more nonlocal cadres had to be sent in. But the party did not want to impose outside leadership on the countryside. As the CCP wrestled with the dilemma, mounting peasant resistance slowed collectivization.

Mao Tse-tung deemed matters so serious that he feared village leadership was about to slip from the party's hands. This was not only a political question; economic growth was at stake. Following the Soviet example, agriculture was supposed to pay for industrialization. But the harvests of 1953 and 1954 were inadequate; land reform may have been a political success, but the system of small peasant ownership was not sufficiently expanding farm production. With the Five-Year Plan already under way, more agricultural growth was urgently needed. Furthermore, "rich peasants" were gaining too much influence in the countryside to suit many CCP leaders. By the spring of 1955 the party, after a long debate, decided that the pace of collectivization would be quickened in order to assert party control at the village level; recruitment of cadres in the countryside would be vastly intensified; the search for village activists, common in Yenan and immediate post-1949 days, would be resumed on a much larger scale; and cadres would go from *hsien* and townships not merely to work in the villages, but to be based in the villages and, in Mao's words, to "become the principal force there." In July Mao announced that within fourteen months the number of households in cooperatives would be doubled, but after five months he announced that the goal had been reached and that a still higher goal was within reach. A "higher stage" of the APC was to be created, in which the semisocialist cooperatives would be replaced by fully socialist collectives; the peasants were to become wage laborers paid according to work points rather than according to the shares they owned in the cooperative. Exultant, Mao declared that socialism's victory over capitalism was almost complete.

Events did not quite fulfill Mao's prediction, despite the promise of early results. The 1955 harvest was good, and many peasants were responding positively to the first stage of collectivization; but others were not. The local cadres in many villages could not obtain the rich peasants' compliance. Higher-level cadres had to step in and back up the local cadres, and more coercion was required than Mao seems to have expected. The Chinese relied much less on force than the Russians had some twenty or more years earlier, and they were more successful than the Russians were, but still the mass-line method of mobilizing the peasants did not suffice to bring about collectivization. The mass-line method of persuasion obtained enough peasant support, participation, and leadership to carry only about one-third of the peasants through the first stage of collectivization by the spring of 1956. Then signs of recalcitrance began to appear, and by autumn many peasants were refusing to go further. Slaughter of livestock, hoarding of grain, refusal to move from lower-stage to higher-stage cooperatives, protests against abolition of private plots and against the failure of income to rise as promised by the party, and substantial migration to the cities were evidence of peasant dismay.

As early as the summer of 1956, therefore, a strong movement developed in the party to slow collectivization. It is likely that outside events helped along this movement in China's internal affairs, for Khrushchev's assault on Stalin's "cult of personality" earlier that year gave Chinese exponents of collective leadership live ammunition to use against Mao. This current in the party won out in time to dominate the Chinese Communist Party Congress in 1956, where a main theme was the assertion of collective leadership in the party and the consequent downgrading of Mao Tse-tung. Liu Shao-ch'i's report to the Congress left the timing of further collectivization flexible, forbade the use of coercion, and stressed that the peasants would have to see the material benefits of collectivization before it could proceed.

In the summer and fall of 1956, then, China's revolution slowed. In seven years China had moved toward socialism in industry and agriculture, but her stress on the Soviet model had resulted in highly unbalanced development. Gains in industry were not matched in agriculture. Poor harvests in 1956 and 1957 forced the government to give food production a higher priority. A period of what is frequently termed relative "liberalization" or relaxation set in. In September 1957 the government ordered the cooperatives to reduce their size by as much as 40 percent, to use a village of about one hundred families as their basic unit, and to maintain the same size for ten years once it has been fixed. The government also introduced various liberalization measures, including the restoration of private plots and livestock. The heart of new policy was that APCs would conform roughly to villages. If the villages had less than one hundred families, two or more of them could combine. The government was therefore compromising with traditional patterns, since many village boundaries were left undisturbed.

With these modifications, collectivization was completed in 1956 and 1957. It had not brought about the total abolition of private property in the countryside, but it had furthered this fundamental socialist goal. Although there would have to be further campaigns to socialize agriculture completely, collectivization had put the CCP in a stronger position to conduct such campaigns. A sizable corps of cadres had been created and had taken over village leadership. Each village was an organized unit with a planned economy, and there were now perhaps 800,000 such collectives, averaging six hundred to seven hundred people in each. It remained to be seen whether the bureaucratic apparatus that soon appeared in the villages, together with the peasants' devotion to their remaining private plots and free markets, would create more problems for the CCP than collectivization was thought to have solved.

The most dramatic feature of the period of relaxation in 1956 and 1957 was Mao's encouragement to the people to express themselves freely: "Let a hundred flowers bloom, let a hundred schools of thought contend." This invitation, formally extended in May 1956, found few takers until a year later when, after repeated urging and frequent assurances that candid criticisms were welcome and would not bring retribution, a substantial number of people spoke out. Exactly why the CCP chose to invite criticism at this time is by no means clear. Perhaps the invitation was intended as a safety valve by which malcontents could let off steam harmlessly instead of exploding. Some observers think it was a trap to lure dissidents into the open, and a few believe it was an attempt to show that the intellectuals had been won over and did not have serious criticisms to make. Almost all interpreters agree, however, that the leadership was astonished at the breadth and depth of the criticisms that were finally expressed.

If this interpretation is correct, it helps to explain the liberalization period and Mao's reaction to it. The relaxation was justifiable on the grounds that neither the peasants nor the intellectuals were yet fully prepared for socialism. Mao's populism did not blind him to the Marxist dictum that peasants are potential capitalists. He could not have failed to observe the persistence of such bourgeois values as acquisitiveness and pursuit of self-interest. In 1949 Mao had not been pessimistic about eliminating the bourgeois mentality by following the conventional Marxist principle of altering the economic substructure, supplemented by his own combination of persuasion, inducement, and coercion. Changes in production relations, he thought —especially the removal of big landlords and big capitalists from privileged status, the nationalizing of industry and commerce, and the collectivizing of land—would be enough to inculcate antibourgeois values in nearly everyone. Those who resisted, particularly intellectuals, would undergo thought reform and other forms of "socialist education," and most would join in "socialist construction" as they had in the war against Japan. Only when this proved not to be the case did Mao revise his thinking and adopt more drastic policies.

Mao rejected Liu Shao-ch'i's view, expressed to the Congress in 1956, that collectivization should be slowed. In February 1957 Mao admitted that "some things did go wrong" and that "some people have stirred up a miniature typhoon" with their criticisms of cooperative farming. But he insisted that what went wrong was not serious and was due to bad weather and other natural causes (which were, in fact, serious) and to cadre errors. Mao dismissed the difficulties with the observation that "new things always have difficulties and ups and downs to get over as they grow." He would be satisfied to finish establishing cooperatives that year and to consolidate them within another five years. Mao agreed with Liu that it was desirable to raise the peasants' incomes year by year, but he countered forcefully that the peasants had gained a great deal in seven years and that if their standard of living was still low the same was true for everyone else. Clearly Mao saw no reason for a policy that would allow collectivization to proceed at the peasants' own pace, as Liu had suggested.

In the same speech that launched his collectivization counterattack, Mao reiterated his Hundred Flowers invitation. In the context of the CCP's internal disagreement about collectivization and political administration, the puzzling Hundred Flowers policy assumes great importance. The full text of Mao's February speech was not published until June, but it was summarized in the Chinese press during March and April. The press explained that Mao wanted to draw particular attention to the bureaucratic tendencies in the party. Bureaucratism, newspaper readers were told, was the main cause of contradictions between leaders and people, and the way to eliminate such contradictions was by criticism and self-criticism. Thus the press presented Mao's unpublished speech as an invitation to criticize the CCP leadership. And in May 1957 this was what intellectuals finally did. Their criticisms ranged widely, but they concentrated on the theme that the party had deteriorated since 1949 and had become elitist, divorced from the masses.

Much of the criticism sounded as if Mao had expressed it himself. Furthermore, when Mao's February speech was published, it was unusually mild in reference to the intellectuals. He even conceded that thought reform had been "carried on in a somewhat rough and ready way" and that "there are bound to be some who are all along reluctant, ideologically, to accept Marxism-Leninism and communism." Mao had often expressed contempt for intellectuals by comparing them to human dung; to say now that "we should not be too exacting in what we expect of them" was remarkably conciliatory. Thus it may not be too farfetched to interpret the Hundred Flowers policy as Mao's indirect attack on other CCP leaders, although most scholars believe that no CCP leader, including Mao, expected such harsh criticism and that all were shocked. In any case, this attack on the CCP provoked a counterattack by the party.

The CCP had expected a "mild breeze" and "gentle rain" of criticism to bring forth a hundred flowers of fresh ideas; instead, party leaders complained, a storm had come and left only weeds. Uprooting of the weeds began in June and intensified through the end of 1957. Intellectuals, especially members of some minor political parties that had been allowed to exist, were the first targets. Soon the CCP counterattack became a huge antirightist campaign that spread to the government bureaucracy, the army, the countryside, and even the party itself. Among the more than 100,000 "counterrevolutionaries" that the minister of public security claimed to have discovered, about 5,000 were CCP members. Intellectuals were charged with plotting to overthrow socialism and the CCP leadership and to restore capitalism. Army leaders were accused of excessive individualism. And everywhere, even in the countryside, massive campaigns raged against bureaucracy—farmers spoke derisively of "four-armed cadres" who stood in the fields giving orders, jackets slung over their shoulders with the empty sleeves dangling or flapping in the breeze; the sleeves symbolized their nonparticipation in manual labor, much as long fingernails distinguished the traditional gentry from the peasants. The "rightists" had to confess their errors and submit to "reform through labor," which for many meant going to the countryside to work in the fields. Meanwhile CCP leaders convened in September and October 1957 to examine their own errors and achievements and to plan for the future.

As the first Five-Year Plan drew to a close, ending the period formally designated as the "transition to socialism," the CCP leaders confronted hard decisions. The basic decision was whether the second Five-Year Plan, scheduled to begin in 1958 and to initiate the "construction of socialism," should follow the pattern of the first. The first had produced highly unbalanced development from 1953 to 1957. Industry had grown enormously, but agriculture had barely kept pace with the increase in population. Without a larger agricultural surplus, there would be insufficient capital to invest in industry. Concessions to the peasants in 1956 had increased the surplus but had also encouraged the reappearance of bourgeois traits in the countryside; since China's goal was not merely to industrialize but to transform society, an industrialization policy that encouraged capitalist traits was self-defeating. Furthermore, some leaders agreed that the plan's emphasis on heavy industry, which required large amounts of capital, was not as suitable for China as it had been for Russia. China had little capital but many people; many smaller plants that relied mostly on manpower made more sense than a few huge plants that relied mostly on machinery. Smaller plants could be scattered around the country and could reduce the centralized planning and management that made for a top-heavy bureaucracy.

The CCP Central Committee, following this reasoning, decided to adopt a policy that more evenly balanced industry and agriculture, heavy industry and light, and centralized planning and local initiative. For example, although iron and steel production remained a high priority goal, much iron and steel was now to be produced locally in small plants. Furthermore, central government bureaus, such as the one responsible for keeping statistics, were broken up into local agencies. An administrative system was to be created in the countryside that combined all functions, from industry and agriculture to education and self-defense, in a new unit that came to be called the commune. Indeed, the commune can be understood as an effort to break down the barriers between city and countryside by transferring to the rural areas much of the work that had been done in the cities. The commune was the culmination of a sporadic but ever-widening expansion of cooperatives that had been under way from as early as 1950 and that Mao now refused to let slacken in 1957. To assure adequate work at local levels, a purge of local officials was conducted (unlike Stalin's purges, it was not bloody), and heavy emphasis was placed upon the participation of the masses.

Early in 1958 this set of policies was ratified by the National People's Congress and soon came to be known as the Great Leap Forward (GLF). The GLF adopted specific national goals, such as surpassing British industrial production within fifteen years, and the "general line" of "going all out, aiming high and achieving greater, faster, better, and more economical results in building socialism." Mao was aiming not only at economic goals, but also at setting in motion "permanent revolution" and driving the country swiftly into full communism.

Huge increases in production were called for beginning in 1958, and targets were steadily raised until the country experienced virtually an epidemic of near-Utopian optimism. Even the Association of Chinese Paleontologists vowed that its scientists would cut thirteen years off their twenty-year targets and would reach in seven years a higher level of research than paleontologists in capitalist countries. No one scene better evokes the mass quixotism to which the Great Leap Forward eventually led than that of scores of paleontologists hastening their pursuit of fossils in order that China might leap into the future.

The fundamental idea on which the seemingly impossible dreams of the Great Leap Forward rested was that China's problems were more political than economic or technological. Problems were to be solved primarily by cultivating proper political attitudes and engaging in correct political action. Lethargic agricultural production, for example, could be blamed only in part on shortages of chemical fertilizer, antiquated farming methods and tools, exhausted soil, and other technical barriers; the more fundamental obstacle was the tendency of some peasants to lapse into capitalistic thinking. During the GLF, therefore, "socialist education" was intensively carried on even in the countryside. A national example was made of one poor peasant who was said to have benefited from land reform but then fallen victim to a bourgeois mentality; soon the nation was flooded with stories explaining how he had begun to seek personal profit and to neglect his assignments in the cooperative and how he had been saved by the quick and effective work of good local cadres. Thus economic backwardness was to be overcome by intensified political effort, heightened class consciousness, and unyielding class struggle against bourgeois influences.

The main slogan of the Great Leap Forward was Politics takes command. In its earliest and simplest form this slogan meant that political authority had to prevail over technical expertise. An alternate slogan was The redder, the more expert. This slogan meant that political reliability and even sheer enthusiasm were preferred to what was scorned as "the fetishism of technology." It was thought better, for example, to have enthusiastic peasants attempt to produce steel in numberless, amateurish backyard furnaces than to turn industry over to technical experts and managerial personnel. Experts and managers, together with urban party members, were ordered to engage regularly in manual labor in order to get closer to the masses. Thousands of cadres were "sent down" first to lower levels of the bureaucracy (from province to *hsien* or from *hsien* to township) and then to production work in cooperatives. The policy was known in Chinese as *hsia-fang,** the literal meaning of which is "downward transfer." Although *hsia-fang* was reminiscent of James Yen's *hsia-hsiang* idea, the CCP's "to the village" movement of the early 1940s, and even earlier CCP practices, its scope was far greater. To demonstrate that *hsia-fang* was important and applicable to all, high officials such as the first secretaries of province committees went out to plow fields and to carry earth. The mayor of Peking worked on a road repair gang and pointed out that he was following a tradition established in Yenan. Indeed, Mao Tse-tung himself is known to have cultivated a vegetable garden in Yenan, and in 1958 he participated in the construction of a reservoir.

---

* Pronounced *hsee-ah fong*.

By February 1958 it was reported that 1.3 million cadres had undergone *hsia-fang*. Up to this time, a major purpose for *hsia-fang* was to redistribute cadres within the top-heavy administrative system. It may also have been intended to send trained personnel out to the countryside as part of the general decentralization, and to reverse what had become a steady and heavy flow of population into the cities. In the spring *hsia-fang* was turned into an even broader effort to bridge social gaps. *Hsia-fang,* purposefully and systematically, was to wipe out the difference between mental and manual labor in all of Chinese society. Not only party cadres and government bureaucrats, but all nonmanual workers were to be "sent down." Another million people, mostly urban intellectuals who lacked experience in manual labor, were sent to work in farms and factories for an entire year. In September the party announced that henceforth "workers of all government organizations, troops, enterprises and industries, except those too old or too sick to take part in physical labor . . . shall spend at least one month a year in physical labor." There could no longer be any doubt that the Chinese revolution was accelerating; bureaucratism and bourgeois values were once again under direct frontal assault.

As the assault got under way during late 1957 and early 1958, the new emphasis on agriculture gave high priority to irrigation and water conservation projects. Following the principle of decentralization, Peking assigned these projects to the APCs, but many of the projects were too big to be handled by one APC. Individual APCs, therefore, began to join forces. Some groups of APCs then found that their labor could be used more efficiently when several groups worked together. Probably with the permission of top-level CCP leaders, and perhaps even at their instigation, APCs began to amalgamate in order to handle other big projects. As the Great Leap Forward gathered speed in the spring of 1958, the APCs assumed still more tasks, including the establishment of small industries. Amalgamation of APCs increased accordingly, even though party leaders cautiously regarded this expansion as an experiment. In July the combined APCs began officially to be called "people's communes," signifying that the CCP had abandoned its earlier policy of keeping APCs relatively small. In August, when nearly a third of the peasants were already in communes, the CCP adopted the system as national policy; by the end of September the figure had leaped to 98 percent. Within a few months China's countryside had been reorganized into some 26,000 communes, averaging about five thousand families in each.

Mao Tse-tung hailed the commune movement unreservedly. Much as the peasants had captured his imagination in 1927, the euphoria of the Great Leap Forward now caught him up. Many times in the thirty-one years since he had discovered the peasants' potential he had been disappointed in them, and on occasion he had pointedly criticized the farmers' attachment to their small holdings, but the rapid amalgamation of the APCs revived his faith. As in Yenan days, the impossible came to seem possible once the unlimited potential of the masses was tapped. In a now famous metaphor he likened the masses to a blank sheet of paper that "has no blotches, and so the newest and most beautiful words can be written on it, the newest and most beautiful pictures can be painted on it." In September 1958, following a cross-country inspection trip, Mao jubilantly announced: "During this trip I have witnessed the tremendous energy of the masses. On this foundation it is possible to accomplish any task whatsoever."

No doubt Mao hoped that the establishing of the communes would resolve the prolonged debates in the CCP about the proper size and relationship of administrative districts and economic units. The basic principle was simply to integrate them, which was in effect little more than a recognition of what had already occurred under collectivization. This principle, however, left room for communes of different sizes, depending upon which level of government the commune absorbed. In most instances the communes were the size of townships, but some communes were the size of *hsien*. But as Mao himself later admitted, size became an end in itself. Forced into what G. William Skinner terms a "grotesquely large mold," the communes failed to align themselves with the traditional socioeconomic pattern of rural trade. As a result, the rapid growth of huge communes seriously disrupted the distribution of goods, and further realignments of administrative and economic functions became necessary. These realignments were accomplished only in 1960 and 1961, after the GLF had been abandoned.

Another objective of communization was to reverse the flow of people from rural to urban areas. During the first Five-Year Plan there had been a vast migration of rural people to the cities, where industry was growing, jobs were available, and wages and living standards were thought to be much higher. This trend, which was already visible when the Communists came to power in 1949, became a near avalanche in 1954 due to food shortages. Repeated efforts failed to stem the tide of migrants. In 1956, for example, Shanghai received more than 500,000 peasants. Government leaders complained of an excessive drain on urban food supplies and sent huge numbers of migrants back to the countryside, but more continued to pour into the cities. By the end of 1957 a total of 8 million migrants had been added to the urban populations despite the expulsions. In 1958 the CCP, admitting that something else had to be tried, decided to build small-scale industries in the countryside and, in general, to develop a diversified local economy that would employ the peasants where they lived. This decision became an important aim of the Great Leap Forward and the commune system. Nevertheless that year another 10 million peasants poured into the cities to find work.

The balance between industry and agriculture had also suffered from a serious decline in rural handicrafts. Toward the end of the first Five-Year Plan, many craftsmen gave up their trades in favor of full-time farm work. A major reason for this was resentment against the hasty manner in which handicraft cooperatives had been founded and, it seems, mismanaged by inexperienced cadres. By the end of 1957 there were nearly 2.5 million fewer craftsmen than three years earlier, a drop of more than 26 percent. Since agricultural production was almost totally dependent on rural handicrafts for many essential farm implements, a continuation of this trend would have been disastrous. During the Great Leap Forward, therefore, an attempt was made to replace the handicraft cooperatives and, most important, to base them in the communes.

The policies of the Great Leap Forward were designed to meet specifically Chinese economic problems. In the first Five-Year Plan the Chinese had followed an essentially Soviet model of central planning, maintaining a distinction (albeit a gradually blurring one) between political administration and economic organization and attempting to substitute capital for labor by investing in heavy industry and mechanizing agriculture. In 1957 and 1958 the Chinese abandoned this Soviet model and began to study their own conditions once again. For example, in China labor was plentiful and capital scarce. As the population raced toward 700 million, China's problem was to find productive employment for her people, not to limit her population or invent labor-saving devices. Thus a birth control program that was introduced in 1955 was abandoned in 1958, in accordance with Mao's conviction that, if proper attitudes of thrift and selflessness were cultivated, resources properly exploited, and production increased, a population of a billion people could be maintained at a satisfactory standard of living by the end of this century. Properly organized, he insisted, China's labor supply would prove not to be excessive.

Reasoning thus, Mao encouraged the building of countless small blast furnaces, which were made of crude clay and bricks and used all available ore, coal, and household scraps such as old pots and pans for raw materials. The "backyard furnace" campaign was scoffed at by contemporary Western observers and has been acknowledged by economists (including the Chinese themselves) to have produced iron and steel that were often inadequate for modern industrial purposes. The backyard furnaces may well have been an absurdity. Most of them were soon abandoned. On the other hand, Edgar Snow, a well-informed journalist who visited China in 1960, observed that "quite a few, with improved methods, continue to produce iron for locally forged agricultural tools." Snow also learned that the experiment provided a training ground for workers and metallurgists who then built small modern plants which, he argues, may make a great deal of sense "for capital-poor underdeveloped countries with limited transport facilities bent on speedy acquisition of a heavy industry."

The backyard furnace campaign is one of the best illustrations of what the commune system was intended to do. For Mao it had not only tangible potential as a training ground, but also the psychological value of involving the masses in new and daring enterprises. Dare to struggle, dare to win, an old Maoist slogan from guerrilla warfare days against the Japanese war machine, was also an attitude to be cultivated in the production struggle.

However Utopian its goals, the Great Leap Forward was inspired by more than blind optimism. It was based on the rational economic choice of refusing to let the central government absorb the surplus that the first Five-Year Plan had produced; instead the surplus was to go to the collectives (or communes) to invest in the development of local resources. Mao's argument, as Jack Gray points out, "was that the peasants would see more point in economic development if they conducted it for themselves as far as possible."

A decentralized economy also made good military sense since it would be much less vulnerable to air attack and to invasion than would an urbanized, concentrated, industrial economy; thus it fitted in with Mao's idea of guerrilla defense and with China's military situation vis-à-vis her major potential military foes. It is questionable whether this was an important consideration at the time the Great Leap Forward was being planned, because Mao was convinced that the launching of the Russian Sputnik in 1957 had given "the Socialist camp" a decisive military lead; however, there are strong indications that Mao was uncertain of Soviet support at this time because of a serious disagreement between the Soviet leadership and himself during his visit to Moscow in November of 1957.

In addition to reasons of economics and military security, the Great Leap Forward in general and the commune system in particular were defensible as programs suited to China's political and social needs. Politically, they attempted to bridge the gap between city and countryside and ease China's eternal tension between centralization and local initiative. Socially, they sought to overcome the distinction between mental and manual labor, a distinction that had been openly sanctioned ever since the great philosopher Mencius explained it in the fourth century B.C.: "Those who labor with their minds rule others; those who labor with their hands are ruled by others."

If there is this much to be said for the rationality of the Great Leap Forward, the obvious question is, Why did it collapse so rapidly and so disastrously? It should be stressed that most scholars do not agree that the Great Leap Forward was a rational program. This is particularly true if rationality is understood to mean the choice of the means that are most appropriate to achieving a desired objective, and if the primary objective of Chinese policy has been economic development in general and industrialization in particular. Economists tend to regard the methods of the Great Leap, particularly the heavy reliance on labor mobilization, as far from the most appropriate means to industrialization. Most probably agree with Ta-Chung Liu: "The Great Leap Forward was based on a sound diagnosis of the basic weakness of the mainland economy but a serious misconception of the proper way to deal with it." The poorly conceived treatment included excessive regimentation of rural life, impossibly long working hours, removal of incentives (such as private plots), unworkable farming and water control techniques, excessive pressure on industrial enterprises to expand production, and "total mis-calculation of technical possibilities in introducing the backyard furnaces." He also notes that the Great Leap Forward happened to meet with bad weather conditions, which contributed to the agricultural disaster from 1958 to 1960, and concludes: "The whole economy suffered a serious leap backward from 1958 to 1961."

Of the reasons given for the economic failures of the Great Leap Forward, the one that is most often cited to explain other failures is regimentation. Even those scholars who are least critical of the Great Leap Forward find that the creation of a massive popular militia was among the most striking features of the program and that the "militarization of the peasantry" was the single most distinctive characteristic of the communes. As the CCP journal *Red Flag* explained, rapid development of agriculture required working people to "act faster, in a more disciplined and efficient way, [so] that they can better be shifted around within a broad framework, like the workers in a factory or the soldiers in a military unit."

The crucial step toward militarization of the peasantry came at the very beginning of the Great Leap Forward, when a vast nationwide movement mobilized labor for waterworks and irrigation projects. Although it began as a village-level system in which people who knew each other worked in small groups in their own areas, it soon grew until brigades of irrigation workers were being shifted from place to place. Peasants were forced to be absent from their villages, because they were engaged in irrigation projects elsewhere, when they were needed for spring planting at home. Some cooperatives tried to solve this problem by forming other specialized brigades (following the example of those engaged in water projects) to perform tasks such as wet-rice transplanting, fertilizer accumulating, or well-digging. As a result, instead of each peasant doing all or many kinds of work in his own cooperative, he did one kind of work in many. The practice amounted to organizing village work as if villages were factories, and it set a pattern for the communes. It also meant for most Chinese peasants the most wrenching break with the past they had ever known. Schurmann has written:

The peasant found himself working on strange land, unfamiliar to him. The intimate knowledge of his own land meant nothing to him any longer. Whereas earlier he could cope with the idiosyncrasies of land according to his "particularistic" knowledge, now nothing but the "universalistic" methods of rationally defined work were left to him. Work became mechanistic, and subject to the commands of cadres who undoubtedly had "general" knowledge of farm processes, but could never match the intimate knowledge of the "old peasant."

It seems highly significant that some of the least successful policies of the Great Leap Forward were those that struck at the foundations of traditional rural life and resembled Soviet policies. Although the GLF policies abandoned the Stalinist model of industrialization, some features of communization were similar to Russian collectivization; as an example, the Russians considered the state farm to be "a factory in the field" and, like the Chinese, sought to convert peasants into rural proletarians.

The commune system foundered on such efforts to re-channel some of the deepest currents in Chinese life. Probably the most disastrous of these experiments was the sudden attempt in August 1958 to introduce an entirely new marketing system in the countryside. Virtually overnight the complex structure of traditional periodic markets, about 90 percent of which were still functioning, was to be replaced by a system of supply and marketing departments within each commune. As a result, the distribution of goods came to a nearly complete halt. Food, clothing, farm tools, and fertilizer became scarce, while food rotted and other goods piled up at shipping points. Desperate emergency measures and improvisations helped bring rural people through one cold and hungry winter, and then rural markets were reestablished. Some ancient practices, it appears, were best left alone.

The same lesson was learned when cadres attempted to redesign the old marketing systems in order to fit the system of political administration. Cooperatives, which were now roughly equivalent in size to the old villages, were to trade with their *hsien* capitals instead of with the old market towns. In many cases this was grossly inefficient and impractical. One cooperative, for example, that had traditionally dealt with a market town which was only two days' travel away, now had to trade with a *hsien* capital that was ten days away. Not until 1962 were such unreasoned departures from traditional practices fully abandoned.

Mao Tse-tung's defense of the GLF was that flaws of this kind were fatal only because China suffered exceptionally unfavorable weather conditions over an extended period of time; the flaws were not inherent in the program, but were amenable to correction. Mao felt that the party cadres were at fault. Regimentation was *their* doing; it was cadre "commandism" and a failure to implement the mass line that were responsible. Cadres mistakenly followed a policy of "the bigger the better"; this too was not inherent in communization. The cadres' excessive enthusiasm and incompetence were responsible for false reporting of production that misled planners at higher levels. Uncontrolled desires to overfulfill quotas also led to such incidents as the dismantling of office heaters and other equipment in order to win a scrap collection drive competition, or the circulation of false rumors that rice and clothing were soon to be supplied freely to each person according to need instead of according to work—that is, that full communism was soon to replace socialism. (One Chinese publication of 1958, however, says Mao himself was responsible for initiating this particular rumor.) Thus the argument can indeed be made that the Great Leap Forward was reasonably well conceived, but poorly implemented and beset with unfavorable treatment from natural causes.

Mao Tse-tung's opponents in the party leadership thought that much more was wrong. Many objected to the decentralization concept on which the communes were founded. "Localism," they complained, was already getting out of hand because the APCs were becoming too powerful; the communes made localities even more self-sufficient. Under these conditions, Mao's critics demanded, how was nationwide planning and coordination to be achieved? Some even felt that "local patriotism" might interfere with national unity.

Party cadres, teachers, students, and other urbanites who were "sent down" to the countryside also objected to Mao's policies. They had expected China's progress to bring the blessings of modern urban civilization to deprived rural folk rather than to convert city intellectuals into farm laborers. Progress was supposed to mean less manual labor, not more. Especially to those trained abroad, possession of technical expertise was thought to make a man more valued, not more suspect of having bourgeois leanings.

Others objected to the lower priority given to heavy industry and the new emphasis on handicrafts, light industry, agriculture and farm-related matters such as water control. Still others objected to the return to a people's militia, some because the militia seemed incompatible with modern military methods, and some because it led to a militarized peasantry and a misplaced confidence in the ability or wisdom of the masses. Finally, there were many who were troubled by the Soviet Union's disapproval of the communes and of Mao's premature claims that China was about to enter the stage of pure communism, particularly since that disapproval led to the withdrawal of Soviet technical advisers and the worsening of Russian-Chinese relations.

Outspoken criticisms of the Great Leap Forward program during most of 1958 forced numerous party conferences to be held. Finally, at the end of the year, a retreat was begun. In December 1958, after only five months of existence, the growth of the communes was checked, and Mao resigned as chairman of the People's Republic of China but not as head of the party. Retrenchment prevailed well into 1959. By late summer, however, Mao had prepared a counterattack. In August, even as the party was admitting catastrophic defeats in the Great Leap and revising downward its production targets for 1959, Mao launched an antirightist campaign. The campaign was directed primarily at those who denied that the masses could handle the tasks of revolutionary construction, who criticized mass movements while failing to participate in them, and who minimized achievements but magnified shortcomings. In brief, the rightists were those opposed to Mao. The campaign continued through October, by which time a second leap was under way, indicating that Mao may have temporarily regained command. Although Mao persevered through 1960, by the end of the year his influence had declined again. The Great Leap Forward was rejected, and in January 1961 liberalization policies were adopted, particularly to stimulate food production. "Experts" who could improve production were now valued over the reddest of the red.

The CCP reversed its communization policy, but it

maintained the form by subdividing communes into production brigades and teams instead of dismantling them. In effect, the CCP went back, not to traditional administration, but to a system in which the commune conformed roughly to the township. The 24,000 huge communes organized at the peak of the Great Leap Forward were broken up into about 74,000 smaller ones, close to the number of townships that existed in 1958. Commune and township boundaries were remarkably similar. At lower levels, however, the production brigades were not as small as the old villages, and the production teams were not as large as the old villages. The teams, which averaged about forty households, became the basic unit in which important decisions were made. The brigade, which was supposed to include no more than ten teams, had the chief responsibility for annual planning and allocated work to the teams. Thus power to organize production and distribute income devolved steadily down to the lower levels. Families were allowed small private plots, and even when working in the production team they usually farmed the same land they had always farmed. The communes, made up of one to two dozen brigades, retained a variety of functions much like the old *hsien*—such as registry of births, deaths, and marriages, and regulation of civil disputes—and they also were to coordinate brigade plans, manage schools and hospitals, and organize other enterprises that were too large for the brigades. The end of the Great Leap Forward, therefore, found the communes far from moribund. Indeed, they made a valuable contribution in the battle waged against flood and drought in 1959 and 1960. But in the winter of 1960–1961, China was far from communism and deep in crisis.

TOWARD PROLETARI-ANIZATION
From 1961 to 1965 the Chinese Communist Party, now dominated by Liu Shao-ch'i, gathered back into its hands much of the power Mao Tse-tung had attempted to disseminate among the masses. The party restored centralized rule, incentives to produce food and other consumer goods, and general policies designed to promote strict but orderly governmental and economic rehabilitation. The single most characteristic emphasis of CCP policy in this period was

the assignment of first priority to economic growth. As one leader close to Liu put it, "No matter whether cats are black or white, as long as they can catch mice they are good cats." Anything that could restore the crippled economy to health, he implied, would be attempted.

Mao found these policies intolerable. Once again, as in 1956 and 1957, he saw the return of a "rich-peasant mentality" in the countryside and a "bureaucratic mentality" in the CCP. Having been relegated at the end of 1958 to a lesser position in the leadership, he lost little time in turning to the army as a new source of power. Indeed, even the abortive revival of the Great Leap Forward in 1959 and 1960 can probably be traced to Mao's success in finding allies among the military.

The temporary return to Mao's policies in the autumn of 1959 followed a sharp internal dispute that resulted in dismissals of high military officials. The minister of defense was replaced by Lin Piao* (1907———), who soon became Mao's closest ally. Signs of an alliance between Mao and Lin multiplied in 1960: a renewed stress on the importance of militia forces and "people's war," the publication of some long-withheld writings by Mao that stressed the relevance of guerrilla strategy to present and future needs, and a revival with unprecedented intensity of a drive to put "politics in command" in the army. The embryonic alliance between Mao and Lin was insufficient to prevent the party's abandonment of Maoist policies in 1961, but as Liu Shao-ch'i and his comrades in the CCP leadership led China out of the "three bad years" (1959–1961), Mao and Lin prepared to renew the struggle for power. Their efforts consisted largely of a nationwide socialist education campaign, especially among soldiers and youth, to propagate Mao's thought.

The campaign was designed to promote Maoist "democracy" among the troops, which meant bringing them closer to the masses. One way to do so was to involve the army in the economy; PLA officers were assigned to business and financial offices, and many economic officials were sent to PLA units for political training. The campaign was

---

* Pronounced *Lin Bee-ow* (rhymes with "now").

also intended to train the young to be the next generation of national revolutionary leaders. Soldiers and revolutionary youth were proclaimed the hope of the future. As the campaign gained momentum in 1963 and 1964, two themes emerged. One theme exposed wrongdoing by party cadres, especially those who were found to have committed "unclean" acts of mismanagement and corruption in the countryside; the other hailed the army as a model for all kinds of work, organization, and behavior. Having profited from more than three years of intensive training in Mao's thought, the army was allegedly immune to the bourgeois germs that were infecting civilian life. The campaign to Learn from the People's Liberation Army peaked in 1964, when the press was saturated with stories of selfless heroism and virtuous acts performed by model soldiers and even by entire units.

The contrast between party cadres who were attacked in 1964 because they were "unclean" and soldiers who were lionized because they served the people and gave no thought to personal gain reveals the underlying struggle that led to the Great Proletarian Cultural Revolution (GPCR). "The party," Jack Gray has written, "is the engine of social change; it cannot just idle, it must pull." If the CCP did not generate social change, Mao feared, China could slip back into what he considered decadent bourgeois democracy. Mao held that precisely such backsliding was occurring in the Soviet Union: The flowering of Soviet "revisionism" was proof that a socialist revolution could be reversed. In the CCP it was apparent, as Michel Oksenberg wrote, that "the zeal for achieving social change has been sapped by a penchant for bureaucratic behavior: the desire to maximize status while minimizing responsibility, the ability to postpone decision and action until the decision or action is no longer required, and the capacity to build an organizational position impregnable to attack." The party was becoming an entrenched elite much like the old gentry—privileged, accustomed to urban comforts, and insensible to the needs and problems of the peasant masses. The entire revolution was at stake. In January 1965 Mao decided that he had failed to rouse the party to action by means of the socialist education campaign. He later confessed that the party and its major organs of propaganda and information were not responsive to his wishes or orders. A new effort was called for; it was soon launched and became the Great Proletarian Cultural Revolution.

The GPCR was to "use the new ideas, culture, customs, and habits of the proletariat to change the mental outlook of the whole of society" and to "touch people to their very souls." It was to create "new forms of organization . . . to keep our party in close contact with the masses." And it was to revive and expand many of the goals of the Great Leap Forward. All this, Mao hoped, would enable China to overcome the Three Great Differences—the differences (or contradictions) between town and country, industry and agriculture, and mental and manual labor. Once these contradictions were resolved, China would at last be proletarianized, not only in the sense that all Chinese would perform manual labor, but in the sense that all would share a new state of mind. To be proletarian now meant to possess no thought of personal advantage and to be totally dedicated to serving one's comrades. These ideals, however far from realization they may be, showed Mao's major aims, particularly in their thrust toward breaking down elitism.

To underline the contrast between party and army and to provide Mao with support for a new campaign against party bureaucratism, Lin Piao stressed anew that the army would place "continued emphasis on politics" and especially upon the "creative study" of Mao's writings. The most dramatic concrete expression of this renewed emphasis was the decision to abolish ranks, awards, and insignia in the army. During and immediately after the Korean War, which required the Chinese army to depart from its guerrilla methods and organization, numerous Soviet-style changes had been introduced. Although some of these changes had been renounced when the Chinese moved away from Soviet models in the late 1950s, the army kept the elaborate system of ranks, epaulettes, badges, pay differentials, and other such expressions of modern military hierarchy. Now it was decided to revert to the guerrilla model in which the only distinction was between "commanders" (officers) and "fighters" (enlisted men). Furthermore all military personnel would wear the same uniform and simple insignia, a red star on the hat and a red badge on the collar. The Russian-style organization, it was explained, had contributed to "class consciousness and ideas to gain fame and wealth." By learning from the People's Liberation Army, China would learn how to eliminate ranks throughout her government and society; elitist bureaucrats would learn from the masses much as officers learned from the rank and file.

Another major reason for these changes in the army was the war in Vietnam. As United States intervention grew, China's leaders had to consider their country's relationship to the war and, in particular, what to do in case of an American attack. Some army and party leaders wanted a build-up of conventional forces and a rapprochement with the Soviet Union that would allow China to obtain modern weapons from her erstwhile ally. Mao and Lin spurned the idea that weapons were decisive and that China needed to rely on the Soviet Union; they favored a "people's war" strategy, in which the political organization and ideological conviction of Chinese guerrillas would count for more than missiles. This issue, which resembled the "expert versus red" issue that divided China's leaders in matters concerning economic development and party and government operations, came to a head in 1965. Once again, a threat from outside coincided with internal turmoil to produce a dual crisis.

Mao left Peking, where he lacked a following, and mobilized support among the youth and the military in order to recapture the party and reconvert it to an engine of revolution. One of Mao's major instruments was the Red Guards. These were organizations of high school and college students that began to form in May 1965. At first they had many names and varied purposes, but they began to gain prominence in June for their unanimous criticism of school and university administrators, "old-fashioned" teachers, and bourgeois students. By August huge numbers of youth had joined Red Guard organizations and sworn allegiance to Mao's crusade.

When Mao felt his support was sufficient, he launched a

political struggle against the underlings of his opponents in Peking; when he felt he had weakened them enough, he returned to Peking and called a meeting of the Central Committee. Amid bitter wrangling Mao pushed through a sixteen-point program for the Cultural Revolution that was issued as a "Decision of the Central Committee of the CCP." This meant that Mao could now issue directives in the name of the Central Committee; it remained to be seen whether he could enforce them.

Mao's struggle went on for about three years and was inseparable from the Great Proletarian Cultural Revolution. The GPCR was both a gigantic struggle for power and, as its name indicates, an immense revolutionary movement aimed at creating a proletarian culture. The sixteen-point program, which may be considered the first full statement of the GPCR's purposes, announced a campaign both to take power from Mao's opponents and to resist the capitalist tendencies they were accused of promoting. To achieve his aims, Mao risked destruction of the CCP.

The wholesale purge of party members at all levels and the prolonged bitter attack on old comrades at the highest levels during the GPCR, although they resulted from at least a decade of disagreement, came as shattering blows to a party that had survived forty-five years of extraordinarily arduous struggle. Explosive mass movements, such as those of the Red Guards, sometimes resulted in injury and deep humiliation to innocent people. The factionalism that became endemic between 1965 and 1968 divided the country as it had not been divided for twenty years: Rival groups of Red Guards fought each other; some military commanders aligned themselves with anti-Mao party officials; others supported pro-Mao Red Guards against party officials; and Mao's wife, who had become very active in his behalf, called for attacks on "the handful of power holders in the army." No group was immune to strife.

As disorder spread to, if not indeed over, the brink of civil war, the crucial political issue in China became the old one of central-local relationships. In 1968, when divisions began to be healed, the army played a decisive role; by September of that year, every province had a new Revolutionary Committee to head its administration, and in nearly every committee the army was dominant. The army itself, however, was no longer unified. Many of its regional commanders, who were now provincial leaders, did not share Mao's beliefs. Mao had defeated his enemies in the party and regained control of it, but the unity of the party and the party's authority in the nation had not yet been restored.

From 1969 to 1971 China moved steadily toward restoring unity in the nation. A clear sign of the beginning of a new era was the convening of the Ninth Party Congress in April 1969. (Only two other congresses had been held since 1928: the Seventh in 1945 and the Eighth in 1956.) The Ninth Party Congress marked the end of the turbulent phase of the Great Proletarian Cultural Revolution. Although the GPCR was not considered over, the Congress declared that production was as necessary as revolution. In another step to promote unity, the Congress called for leniency toward Mao's defeated opponents; they were to be given the opportunity to reform and make a fresh start. Chou En-lai has said that less than 1 percent of the party members were expelled, although many were sent to the countryside for "reform through labor."

In the months following the Ninth Congress, the CCP made a major effort to rebuild itself and to restore the power of the central government. Many former party members regained their positions. The central government bureaucracy, which had been reduced by more than 80 percent during and immediately after the GPCR, began to grow again. Peking also asserted its authority over the economy. By the middle of 1971, in addition to suggesting that more centralized political authority was needed, the CCP said that the highly desirable trend toward provincial and regional economic self-sufficiency should be coordinated with the national planned economy according to party directives.

As party rebuilding proceeded in 1971, foreign analysts continued to stress that the army was at least sharing power with the CCP and was possibly the party's rival. The analysts supported their beliefs with the facts that about 40 percent of the members of the Central Committee were military men and that Lin Piao, who had been designated by the new constitution promulgated at the Ninth Party Congress to be Mao's successor, seemed to have fallen from favor or even to have been killed. Chou En-lai, however, minimized the alleged rivalry between party and army. Furthermore, aside from a few spectacular but isolated incidents such as the cancellation of National Day celebrations in 1971, China seemed free of tension and politically quite stable. The more important points about the army seemed to be that its activities were highly diversified—including, for example, medical experimentation and school teaching—and that it was, in the words of a visitor, "an oddly unmilitary army." The military personnel were without rank insignia and wore the same shapeless and rumpled uniforms, symbolizing their egalitarianism and devotion to serving the people; significantly, much was being made of the army's tradition of public service that was built up in the Yenan period.

While the creation of a fully proletarian culture and a new community of 800 million comrades awaits the outcome of political readjustments, social change is proceeding. The keystone of Maoist policy continues to be the interdependence of social and political objectives—to build socialism it is necessary to have a revitalized party, and to have a revitalized party it is necessary to move steadily toward a proletarian society. Thus party rebuilding depends upon reestablishing the party's political strength and upon reducing the Three Great Differences. In Mao's view, the ultimate solution to problems of political unity, social change, and economic development continues to be the commune system, in which a relatively high degree of administrative decentralization encourages the people's sense of participation, releases their energies and productive capacities, and avoids excessive bureaucratization; and ideological solidarity, which means common allegiance to Mao's thought, provides national unity. Indeed, it sometimes seems that ideological unity is intended as a substitute for political and economic centralization. If so, Mao's China bears a certain resemblance to traditional China. But Mao believes that only the commune system can permanently eliminate the Three Great Differences, and while the commune system awaits full renewal and flowering, there can only be piecemeal progress toward reducing them. Meanwhile the campaign to promote ideological unity goes on unabated.

To persuade China's millions that their destiny is in their own hands, Mao's thought carries an essentially simple and direct message, designed to give courage and confidence to an impoverished and pessimistic people: Ordinary men can do extraordinary things, whether defeating a modern mechanized army or making steel. The highly intensive campaign to study Mao's thought, a drive that swept China during the Great Proletarian Cultural Revolution, was an effort to create all across the nation an atmosphere of striving, perseverance, and confidence. The glorification of Mao is not an unimportant by-product of this ideological campaign, but it seems distinctly subordinate to the aims of promoting solidarity and optimism.

The campaign to glorify Mao and his thought has gone hand in hand with bold but risky experiments, such as those in education and medicine, aimed at reducing the Three Great Differences and building a proletarian culture. Education, which for decades had been criticized by reformers for its preoccupation with arts, letters, and remote antiquity and its indifference to problems of food production and other current matters of life and death to millions of people, was for a time delivered almost entirely into the hands of the untrained. As the GPCR wound to an end, schools which had been closed during the height of it reopened under the complete control of workers and poor and lower-middle peasants. In cities, factories ran the schools near them; big factories ran secondary schools, and medium and small factories ran primary schools. In the countryside, peasants ran the schools. These "bare-foot teachers," as they were called, included old farmers, educated youth, and demobilized PLA soldiers. They taught not only the children but also former professional teachers. Those teachers were expected to "be pupils before they become teachers" and were sent to live, labor, learn, and "combat self-interest and repudiate revisionism" under the peasants' tutelage. Schools have increasingly become adjunct to factories and farms. Students do part-time work and spend less time than formerly in classrooms and libraries. Those high school graduates who go on to college are now expected first to spend three years doing manual labor.

In 1970, as many universities reopened doors that had been closed for more than four years, some concessions were offered to professional teachers, but they were still criticized for old failings. Too many, it was charged, cling to familiar routine, avoid political activity, divorce theory from practice, and "worship things foreign." * To cure these ills it is now planned that universities will be reorganized according to a "three-in-one" system that combines teaching, research, and production. At Tsinghua University, which is intended to be a model for others, several factories have been established to manufacture goods that are urgently needed by industry and the military, the production of which meets teaching and research needs. Students are recruited from experienced and activist workers, peasants, soldiers, and cadres, whose knowledge of class struggle and production will enable them to teach teachers as well as learn from them.

The "bare-foot teachers" have their counterpart in medicine, where a campaign to train "bare-foot doctors" began at least as early as 1965. At that time Mao issued a directive on public-health work criticizing its failure to treat the masses. Mao complained that medical education took too long because it wasted too much time. Citing the examples of two famous doctors from antiquity who were successful without formal modern training, Mao called for a program of "learning in actual experience," especially to equip doctors to treat the most common diseases. Mao accused colleges of occupying themselves with "so-called advanced research into abstruse and complicated treat-

---

* These worshippers, interestingly enough, were said to be "obsessed with the slavish comprador ideology of trailing behind at a snail's pace." This phrase recalls a famous turning point in Communist history, for in the late 1920s Bukharin opposed Stalin's collectivization scheme with the view that the peasants should "enrich themselves" and the Soviet Union should "creep at a snail's pace" to socialism. Stalin, however, insisted on amalgamating farms in order to reach socialism as quickly as possible.

ments" and of neglecting to teach diagnosis and treatment of the most common diseases. "The manner in which doctors are being trained is . . . for the purpose of the cities, but there are more than 500 million peasants in China."

Such well-aimed criticisms have occasionally led Mao to rashness. "There is altogether no need to read so many books," he has argued. "The more one reads, the more foolish one becomes." Overstatements of this kind should be understood as part of his broad campaign to combine practice with theory and to give priority to practical experience. The purpose is to develop "people's medicine" and thereby to correct the imbalance that has long existed in China between the concerns of the intellectuals and the needs of the majority of the people.

The "bare-foot doctors" in the country and the "workers' doctors" in the city receive formal medical training for three months and then divide their time between the practice of relatively easy medicine under the supervision of hospital personnel and their former occupation. They later receive advanced medical training for three more months. This training program provides them with enough knowledge to treat routine ailments. More serious medical problems are handled by the commune hospital, and the most difficult by the city hospital. A doctor from the United States who interviewed some of the "bare-foot doctors" in 1971 said that he was "very highly impressed" with their competence.

In view of Mao's reference to Chinese doctors of antiquity, it is especially noteworthy that the new focus on "people's medicine" has encouraged the use of traditional Chinese medicine. The Chinese claim that a new acupuncture method, inspired by Mao Tse-tung's thought as well as by old methods, has "enabled thousands of deaf-mutes to speak and to cheer 'Long live Chairman Mao!'—the most powerful music of our time." Acupuncture is also said to have helped many paralytics to walk and work again and to have made it possible for some who had been blind "to see again and look at the brilliant image of the great leader Chairman Mao." When the glorification of Mao slackened in 1971, the solid scientific substance of the many claims began to emerge from beneath the propaganda. Some of the medical claims have been verified by foreign visitors; in the words of one doctor from the United States who observed acupuncture treatment, "I have seen the past and it works." *

Many of the Chinese claims seem extreme, but the evidence of Chinese scientific and technological excellence mounts steadily. Not all of this progress can be traced to the inspiration of Mao Tse-tung or to the initiative of the masses; the Chinese have also learned from American-trained scientists and Russian advisers. To knowledge gained from outsiders, the Chinese have added their own talents and resources to advance spectacularly in nuclear science and weaponry. In 1964, four years after the Russian advisers left China and nineteen years after the United States exploded the first atomic bomb, the Chinese exploded their first nuclear device, demonstrating a technology more advanced than that of Britain and France. In 1969 came their first H-bomb, only seventeen years after the original, and then a satellite only thirteen years after Sputnik. Each time the Chinese have narrowed the gap, and each time their scientists have surprised scientists elsewhere with their technological sophistication. The evidence of Chinese innovations in other fields is also remarkable. They have developed new farming methods and machinery, new industrial processes, and new surgical techniques such as the restoration of severed arms and legs. Many of these major breakthroughs were made by people who lacked formal or technical training.

Mao's thought has contributed less to these advancements than the Chinese claim, but more than skeptical outsiders think. His teachings that the people must rely on themselves, that they must learn from each other and from their own experience, and that they should not be discouraged by failure, have made a major contribution to the Chinese success. When the sport champions and scientists attribute their success to the teachings of Chairman Mao, they are referring to these principles. With a people

---

* The doctor was recalling the comment of Lincoln Steffens, who, after visiting the Soviet Union in 1919, said, "I have seen the future and it works."

bound by traditional passivity and models of restrained Confucian gentlemen, in a country battered by a century of disasters, such principles had to be taught. But Mao is not the only inspirational model offered to the Chinese people; they are also exhorted to learn from model communes, industries, soldiers, and other model comrades. Teaching and learning by example, a cornerstone of traditional Chinese theory and practice, has been creatively adapted to revolutionary purposes; thus China is modernizing without Westernizing.

The thrust of all such exhortations is to reduce the Three Great Differences and especially to narrow the gap between the intellectuals, specialists, and officials on the one hand and the masses on the other. The new acupuncture treatment, the Chinese say, has done more than cure common diseases: "While ensuring that medical and health work serves the workers, peasants, and soldiers even better, it can also be easily mastered by them." Although it is stressed that "China needs the services of as many intellectuals as possible," it is also stressed that they must be re-educated and transformed by integrating themselves with the peasants. Model intellectuals are those such as the "rusticated cadre" who told how at first he resented being sent to work in the countryside but eventually profited from it.

When I became a cadre, I gradually forgot my source of origin, and divorced myself from the masses. Unintentionally I became lazy; my thinking became revisionist. I was offended by Chairman Mao's call: "send down the broad masses of cadres to do manual work." . . . Since I arrived in the countryside, I have been living, laboring, and fighting together with the poor and lower-middle peasants. . . . Now I am not only physically close to the poor and lower-middle peasants, but my heart is one with the poor and lower-middle peasants.

It is impossible to know how many intellectuals have become model intellectuals. Some have, but others have continued to be recalcitrant. Some young people have resisted going to the countryside, or, having gone, have fled to Hong Kong or back to the cities, or stayed and aroused resentment among the peasants because of their attitudes and limited work skills, or "corrupted" the peasants instead of learning from them. The party has only redoubled its efforts, as suggested by the following editorial:

A special characteristic of intellectuals is that they are cocky. We don't want those intellectuals who smell good, we want those who stink. Only when they know they stink will they feel the need to transform themselves. We hope that these comrades will sincerely go to the countryside to be little pupils of the poor and lower-middle peasants.

*   *   *

The Great Proletarian Cultural Revolution changed China; official publications have even called it "China's second revolution." But China is still at a very early stage in her modern era. With due allowance for the exaggerations of propaganda slogans, the repeated campaigns against "feudalist superstition," "habits from the old society," and "bourgeois ideology" reveal that old problems remain and that cultural change has been far from total. China's leaders freely admit this and foresee that movements like the Great Proletarian Cultural Revolution will be needed again. Mao told a recent visitor that the Chinese peasants have not lost their "spontaneous desire" to become capitalists. China's leaders also concede that the economy is "relatively backward." (The gross national product is about the same as Canada's, although the population is forty times as great.) In 1971, despite what was claimed to be the tenth consecutive good harvest, China's leaders acknowledged that the agricultural productivity was too low and that more mechanization was needed. Foreign visitors have observed insufficient use of chemical fertilizer and the use of primitive farming methods. These and other problems make modernization a continuing struggle. But these problems, however urgent they are, must be weighed against the changes. The last twenty-two years of unprecedented political effort, social change, and industrialization make the twenty-one years of Kuomintang rule appear stagnant in comparison. China is no longer the "living fossil" that Marx saw in 1862; nor can today's revival of selected traditions be derided, as Chiang Kai-shek's New Life Movement was, as a "Return-to-the-Old-Life-Movement." China has become a young and vigorous country.

Experiments proliferate. Policies change. "We have learned that the centralized Soviet model works poorly in China," a party official told a recent visitor. "To govern 800 million people, you have to decentralize." But the search for a viable balance between centralization and decentralization goes on, and the outcome of that search is uncertain. What is certain is that the old relationship between Chinese leaders and followers has been radically changed and that in this former land of continuity, change has become a way of life. China's struggle to modernize is now fully launched.

Epilogue

Modern China
and
World History

The point of departure for this book was the viewpoint of a distinguished Western historian concerning the last few centuries of world history. Those centuries look quite different to a contemporary Chinese student of world history. If he would recognize a "European Age" at all, he would probably allot to it a maximum of one century; the most convenient benchmarks might be the "unequal treaties," first imposed upon China in 1842 and finally abrogated in 1943. If the European Age is conceived of as an era of European cultural influence rather than a period of diplomatic and military dominance, it might be considered (from a Chinese viewpoint) to have spanned even less than a century. European cultural influence on China has a long history, but it is scarcely a significant history until about 1860 at the earliest, and we cannot begin to speak of powerful European cultural influence until the very end of the nineteenth century or the beginning of the twentieth. (Curiously enough, Western culture became important in China almost precisely at the time when Western political-military-economic domination reached its peak and began to decline.) Western culture, which enjoyed an extraordinary vogue in China for the first twenty to thirty years of this century, never came truly to dominate Chinese life, and its influence receded steadily after about 1928.

Nevertheless, that influence has been pervasive and persistent enough to reach China's very marrow and profoundly alter the course of her history. However brief or lengthy the European Age may be considered to have been, even in a Chinese perspective its decisive importance must be acknowledged. But how, after all, is that importance to be described? Although it is proper to ask this question, we are forced to postpone a firm answer. Some will object, on the grounds that an answer is available; communism, it is held, has been a vehicle for a type of Westernization. In this view, China has been not only deeply influenced but overwhelmed by a particular segment of Western culture, that of Marxism-Leninism.

But communism still has a relatively short history in China, and it is far from having taken a permanent shape. Although the Soviet model provided a blueprint to which much of the Chinese system still conforms, forces are at work to keep the Chinese system fluid, and the struggle to refashion its institutional forms shows no sign of slackening. Furthermore, communism's history in China shows a repeated alternation between adherence to a foreign model and adaptation to uniquely Chinese conditions, and there is no reason to think that adaptation is ending.

Communism has furthered many new trends that were already well under way before it arrived in China—for example, a belief in the value of change, youth's demand that the traditional age hierarchy be destroyed, women's insistence on equality between the sexes, the belief in the value of science and technology. Communism has also done much that is entirely new—collectivization, mass mobilization, mass public health and literacy campaigns. On the surface it may appear that the changes fostered by communism so heavily outweigh the continuities in Chinese life that there is little to be gained by comparing them. And yet, continuities often assert themselves in ways that are less tangible, harder to see, and more difficult to measure than membership in the Communist party, literacy, number of scientists, and output of modern industry. Archeological research, reproduction and wide exhibition of ancient art, conversion of imperial palaces into public gardens and museums, glorification of ancient heroes, revival of traditional medicine, survival of Chinese writing, and the persistence of traditional forms in literature are only some of the ties that bind today's China to yesterday's.

These fragile ties are sometimes compared to lifeless museum artifacts—objects of curiosity rather than growing, vital organisms—and sometimes to mere instruments useful to nationalist rulers or culture-destroying cynics. In fact, we cannot measure the weight that such ties to the past carry in Chinese life. We cannot tell whether the cultural pride they encourage also taps a deep longing for an attachment to distinctively Chinese roots. We do not know whether most Chinese couples freely marry with little or no attention to their parents' wishes, nor is it clear to us whether "bureaucratism" so desperately attacked by the Maoists is essentially a residue of China's centuries-old bureaucratism. We do know that attempts to break down old administrative divisions and marketing patterns have been forced repeatedly to retreat from or compromise with ancient habits; attempts to press collectivization have been blocked by old attachments to land and perhaps even by some modern notions of property rights; attempts to impose conformity in thought, which may have some roots in tradition, have encountered opposition from traditional ruses to avoid conformity as well as from modern notions of freedom.

In brief, while it would be exceedingly rash to assert that continuities dominate Chinese life, it would be scarcely less rash to overlook both the extraordinary staying power that Chinese culture has demonstrated for three thousand years and the fact that China's cultural heritage, physical environment, huge population, and ethnic and linguistic diversity place limitations upon the speed of revolutionary change. China and communism have already changed each other; which has changed more remains an open question. A new cultural synthesis will perhaps never finally work itself out, since in the modern world there is never an end to change; but whatever form China's synthesis takes, her modern society will be recognizable as distinctively Chinese.

It may well turn out, therefore, that the impact of Western culture upon China has been in some ways comparable to the impact of the outside world upon late medieval and early Renaissance Europe. "Europe itself," Professor Palmer pointed out, "has always received much from others—from the calendar and Christianity to the use of cotton and potatoes. Europe itself, moreover, became 'modernized' by the effects upon it of its growing contacts with the earth as a whole, especially after the discovery of America and the ocean trade routes in the days of Columbus." Thus Europe, after a long history of borrowing from abroad, came to a point in its history when foreign contact stimulated it to pursue new directions; those directions are perhaps best symbolized by the idea of man's unlimited potential and his Faustian striving. Europeans' striving did not produce uniformly rapid results. Copernicus was only a generation later than Columbus, but Galileo did not appear for another century and Darwin two centuries more; James Watt's steam engine and the Declaration of the Rights of Man and Citizen both appeared about two hundred years ago, but we are still waiting for more than a small fraction of mankind to enjoy the fruits of steam power and human equality. China, sometimes regarded as a "failure" in comparison with Western Europe and Japan, has barely begun her struggle to modernize. If she has accomplished no "miracles" comparable to those achieved by Japan's samurai and industrialists, neither has she visited upon the world anything like the destruction and suffering caused by Japan's militarists, to say nothing of this century's European wars. At this early stage it is enough that, like Europe, China has now been stimulated to pursue new directions and that she is irrevocably committed to the pursuit. Outside stimulation aroused Europe and contributed to a cultural (scientific) revolution, but it did not tear Europe loose from all its roots. Perhaps outside stimulation has similarly revitalized China.

Bibliography

What follows is a short list of basic sources, most of which have been heavily drawn upon for this book. The most important single book on modern China is *Franz Schurmann's *Ideology and Organization in Communist China* (2nd ed., enlarged; Berkeley and Los Angeles: University of California Press, 1968); although it deals primarily with the 1950s, the second edition has a substantial supplement devoted to the 1960s, and the book is so broadly conceived that it bears directly on all of modern Chinese history. Among others that touch upon a wide range of issues, one of the most stimulating is *China in Crisis*, edited by Ping-ti Ho and Tang Tsou (2 vols.; Chicago: The University of Chicago Press, 1968).

Beginning students now have access to a number of excellent collections that combine translations of original Chinese sources and Chinese scholarly writings, original Western-language sources, Western scholarly writings, journalists' accounts, and authoritative editorial commentary. Among these collections the most comprehensive is *The China Reader*, edited by Franz Schurmann and Orville Schell (3 vols.; New York: Random House, Vintage Books, 1967). Of equivalent quality, but less comprehensive, are *The Awakening of China, 1793–1949*, edited by Roger Pelissier (New York: Capricorn Books, 1970); *Sources of Chinese Tradition*, compiled by W. T. deBary, Wing-tsit Chan, and Chester Tan (New York: Columbia University Press, 1960; in the two-volume paperback edition, Volume 2 deals with modern times); *China's Response to the West, A Documentary Survey, 1839–1923*, edited by Ssu-yü Teng and John K. Fairbank (Cambridge, Mass.: Harvard University Press, 1954; New York: Atheneum, 1963); and *China in Revolution*, edited by Vera Simone (New York: Fawcett Books, 1968).

---

* Available in paperback.

Many periodicals include material on China, but the only high-quality scholarly journal devoted entirely to modern China is *The China Quarterly* (London, 1960——). While emphasizing the post-1949 period, it includes material on earlier history, especially the history of Chinese communism, and it contains a valuable section that chronicles and documents current affairs in China. It is indispensable.

Finally, there are several books that deal with a considerable portion of modern Chinese history and do not fit the chapter listings that follow: *Chinese Intellectuals and the West, 1872–1949* by Y. C. Wang (Chapel Hill, N.C.: University of North Carolina Press, 1966); *Biographical Dictionary of Republican China*, edited by Howard L. Boorman and Richard C. Howard (4 vols.; New York: Columbia University Press, 1967–1970); and *Confucian China and Its Modern Fate: A Trilogy*, by Joseph R. Levenson (Berkeley: University of California Press, 1968).

Chapter 1: The Modern World and Nineteenth-Century China

Banno, Masataka. *China and the West, 1858–1861*. Cambridge, Mass.: Harvard University Press, 1964.

* Chang, Chung-li. *The Chinese Gentry*. Seattle, Wash.: University of Washington Press, 1955.

* Ch'u, Tung-tsu. *Local Government in China under the Ch'ing*. Cambridge, Mass.: Harvard University Press, 1962.

* Fairbank, John K. *Trade and Diplomacy on the China Coast*. Cambridge, Mass.: Harvard University Press, 1953.

* Hsiao, Kung-ch'uan. *Rural China*. Rev. ed. Seattle, Wash.: University of Washington Press, 1967.

* Hucker, Charles O. *The Traditional Chinese State in Ming Times*. Tucson, Ariz.: University of Arizona Press, 1961.

Michael, Franz, and Chung-li Chang. *The Taiping Rebellion*. 3 vols. Seattle, Wash.: University of Washington Press, 1966–1970.

Palmer, R. R., and Joel Colton. *A History of the Modern World*. 3rd ed. New York: Knopf, 1961.

* Wright, Mary C. *The Last Stand of Chinese Conservatism*. Palo Alto, Calif.: Stanford University Press, 1957.

Chapter 2: The Swing Toward Westernization, 1900–1928

> Cameron, Meribeth E. *The Reform Movement in China, 1898–1912*. Palo Alto, Calif.: Stanford University Press, 1931.
>
> * Chow, Tse-tung. *The May Fourth Movement*. Cambridge, Mass.: Harvard University Press, 1960.
>
> Gasster, Michael. *Chinese Intellectuals and the Revolution of 1911*. Seattle, Wash.: University of Washington Press, 1969.
>
> * Levenson, Joseph R. *Liang Ch'i-ch'ao and the Mind of Modern China*. Cambridge, Mass.: Harvard University Press, 1953.
>
> * Schiffrin, Harold Z. *Sun Yat-sen and the Origins of the Chinese Revolution*. Berkeley: University of California Press, 1969.
>
> Schwartz, Benjamin. *In Search of Wealth and Power: Yen Fu and the West*. Cambridge, Mass.: Harvard University Press, 1964.
>
> Tretiakov, S. M. *A Chinese Testament*. New York: Simon and Schuster, 1934.
>
> Wright, Mary C. (ed.). *China in Revolution: The First Phase, 1900–1913*. New Haven, Conn.: Yale University Press, 1968.

Chapter 3: Modernization Under the Kuomintang Government, 1928–1949

> * Barnett, A. Doak. *China on the Eve of Communist Takeover*. New York: Praeger, 1963.
>
> Chang, John K. "Industrial Development of China, 1912–1949," *Journal of Economic History*, Vol. 28 (March 1967), 56–81.
>
> * Ch'ien, Tuan-sheng. *The Government and Politics of China*. Cambridge, Mass.: Harvard University Press, 1950.
>
> Chu, Samuel C. "The New Life Movement, 1934–1937." In John E. Lane (ed.), *Researches in the Social Sciences on China*. New York: East Asian Institute, Columbia University, 1957.
>
> * Feuerwerker, Albert. *The Chinese Economy, 1912–1949*. Ann Arbor, Mich.: Center for Chinese Studies, University of Michigan, 1968.

Liu, F. F. [Liu Chih-pu]. *A Military History of Modern China, 1924–1949*. Princeton, N.J.: Princeton University Press, 1956.

Liu, Ta-chung, and Kung-chia Yeh. *The Economy of the Chinese Mainland: National Income and Economic Development, 1933–1959*. Princeton, N.J.: Princeton University Press, 1965.

* North, Robert C. *Kuomintang and Chinese Communist Elites*. Stanford, Calif.: Stanford University Press, 1952.

* Peck, Graham. *Two Kinds of Time*. Boston: Houghton Mifflin, 1950.

Skinner, G. William. "Marketing and Social Structure in Rural China, Part II," *The Journal of Asian Studies*, Vol. 24 (February 1965), 195–228.

Sun Yat-sen. *San Min Chu I, The Three Principles of the People*. Frank W. Price (tr.). Shanghai: The Commercial Press, 1927.

Tung, W. L. *Political Institutions of Modern China*. New York: International Publications Service, 1964.

Chapter 4: The Chinese Communists on Their Way to Power, 1920–1949

* Barnett, A. Doak (ed.). *Chinese Communist Politics in Action*. Seattle, Wash.: University of Washington Press, 1969. See Part One, articles by Roy Hofheinz, Jr., Ilpyong J. Kim, and Mark Selden.

* Chen, Jerome. *Mao and the Chinese Revolution*. New York: Oxford University Press, 1967.

Chesneaux, Jean. *The Chinese Labor Movement, 1919–1927*. Stanford, Calif.: Stanford University Press, 1968.

* Compton, Boyd. *Mao's China: Party Reform Documents, 1942–44*. Seattle, Wash.: University of Washington Press, 1952.

Eto, Shinkichi. "Hai-lu-feng: The First Chinese Soviet Government," *The China Quarterly*, No. 8 (October–December 1961), 161–83; and No. 9 (January–March 1962), 149–81.

* Johnson, Chalmers A. *Peasant Nationalism and Communist Power: The Emergence of Revolutionary China, 1937–1945*. Stanford, Calif.: Stanford University Press, 1962.

Mao Tse-tung. *Selected Military Writings, 1928–1949.* Peking: Foreign Languages Press, 1963.

* Schram, Stuart R. *Mao Tse-tung.* New York: Simon and Schuster, 1967.

* ———. *The Political Thought of Mao Tse-tung.* Rev. ed., enlarged. New York: Praeger, 1969.

* Schwartz, Benjamin. *Chinese Communism and the Rise of Mao.* Cambridge, Mass.: Harvard University Press, 1951.

* Snow, Edgar. *Red Star over China.* New York: Random House, 1938.

Van Slyke, Lyman P. *Enemies and Friends: The United Front in Chinese Communist History.* Stanford, Calif.: Stanford University Press, 1967.

* Whiting, Allen S. *Soviet Policies in China, 1917–1924.* New York: Columbia University Press, 1954.

Chapter 5: The Chinese Communists in Power, 1949–1971

Barnett, A. Doak. *Cadres, Bureaucracy, and Political Power in Communist China.* New York: Columbia University Press, 1967.

* ——— (ed.). *Chinese Communist Politics in Action.* Seattle, Wash.: University of Washington Press, 1969.

Bowie, Robert R., and John K. Fairbank. *Communist China 1955–59, Policy Documents with Analysis.* Cambridge, Mass.: Harvard University Press, 1962.

An Economic Profile of Mainland China. Studies Prepared for the Joint Economic Committee, Congress of the United States. 2 vols. Washington, D.C.: U.S. Government Printing Office, 1967.

Gittings, John. *The Role of the Chinese Army.* London: Oxford University Press, 1967.

Gray, Jack, and Patrick Cavendish. *Chinese Communism in Crisis: Maoism and the Cultural Revolution.* New York: Praeger, 1968.

Hofheinz, Roy. "Rural Administration in Communist China," *The China Quarterly,* No. 11 (July–September 1962), 140–59.

Oksenberg, Michel. "Communist China: A Quiet Crisis in Revolution," *Asian Survey,* Vol. 6 (January 1966), 3–11.

Skinner, G. William. "Marketing and Social Structure in Rural China, Part III," *The Journal of Asian Studies,* Vol. 24 (May 1965), 363–99.

Snow, Edgar. *The Other Side of the River.* New York: Random House, 1962.

* Townsend, James R. *Political Participation in Communist China.* Berkeley and Los Angeles: University of California Press, 1967.

Vogel, Ezra. *Canton under Communism.* Cambridge, Mass.: Harvard University Press, 1969.

* Yang, C. K. *A Chinese Village in Early Communist Transition.* Cambridge, Mass.: The Technology Press, 1959.

Chronology

1839–1860	Period of "opium wars" and "unequal treaties"
1850–1864	T'ai-p'ing Rebellion
1884–1885	China defeated in war with France
1894–1895	China defeated in war with Japan
1897–1898	Foreign powers' rush for colonies in China
1898	Hundred Days' reform, led by K'ang Yu-wei
1900	Boxer Uprising
1905	Abolition of China's traditional civil service examination system; founding of Revolutionary Alliance, led by Sun Yat-sen
October 1911	Outbreak of republican revolution
1912	Abdication of Manchus and establishment of Republic of China
May 1915	Japan presents Twenty-one Demands to China
1919	May Fourth Movement
July 1921	Founding and first congress of Chinese Communist Party
January 1923	Joint statement by Sun Yat-sen and Adolph Joffe; beginning of cooperation between KMT and CCP
1925	May Thirtieth Movement against foreigners in Shanghai
March 1926	Coup by Chiang Kai-shek against Communists in Canton
July 1926	Beginning of Northern Expedition
April 1927	Chiang Kai-shek breaks with KMT left and Communists
November 1927	Mao Tse-tung sets up soviets in Hu-nan
October 1928	Founding of Nationalist government; Chiang Kai-shek president
September 1931	Japan invades Manchuria
November 1931	Founding of the Chinese Soviet Republic in Chiang-hsi province
October 1934	Beginning of the Long March
October 1935	CCP headquarters established in Shen-hsi province, near Yenan
July 1937	Beginning of Sino-Japanese War; second KMT-CCP united front

April 1939	Fighting resumes between KMT and CCP forces
August 1945	War with Japan ends
July 1946	Beginning of civil war
January 1949	End of battle of Huai-hai, last major military engagement of civil war; Communists take Peking
October 1949	Establishment of People's Republic of China
February 1950	Sino-Soviet Pact of Friendship and Alliance, and trade agreement between China and Soviet Union
June 1950	Adoption of land reform law
December 1952	Announcement of first Five-Year Plan to begin in 1953
Summer–Fall 1955	Drive to fulfill targets of Five-Year Plan and promote agricultural cooperatives
May 1957	Hundred Flowers period; three weeks of free expression
June 1957	Beginning of antirightest campaign
August 1957	Beginning of *hsia-fang*; cadres sent to work in factories and villages
Fall 1957	Beginning of decentralization
May 1958	Great Leap Forward policies stated
December 1958	Retreat from Great Leap Forward; Mao resigns as chairman of government
1960 to January 1961	A second Great Leap Forward
November 1965	First signs of Great Proletarian Cultural Revolution
May 1966	GPCR begins in universities
August 1966	GPCR fully under way; Red Guards officially created
April 1967	Campaign against Liu Shao-ch'i officially begins
1968	China governed by "revolutionary committees"
April 1969	Ninth Party Congress
October 1971	People's Republic of China accepts Chinese seat in United Nations

Index

DATE DUE

NOV 28 '88			
SE 26 91			
OC 13 '99			